meatless

more than **200** of the
very best vegetarian recipes

from the kitchens of
martha stewart living

foreword by
MARTHA STEWART

BANTAM PRESS

LONDON · TORONTO · SYDNEY · AUCKLAND · JOHANNESBURG

CONVERSION CHART

Oven temperatures
130°C = 250°F = Gas mark D
150°C = 300°F = Gas mark 2
180°C = 350°F = Gas mark 4
190°C = 375°F = Gas mark 5
200°C = 400°F = Gas mark 6
220°C = 425°F = Gas mark 7
230°C = 450°F = Gas mark 8

American solid measures
1 cup rice US = 225g
1 cup flour US = 115g
1 cup butter US = 225g
1 stick butter US = 115g
1 cup dried fruit US = 225g
1 cup brown sugar US = 180g
1 cup granulated sugar US = 225g

Spoon measures
1 level tablespoon flour = 15g
1 heaped tablespoon flour = 28g
1 level tablespoon sugar = 28g
1 level tablespoon butter = 15g

Liquid measures
1 cup US = 275ml
1 pint US = 550ml
1 quart US = 900ml

TRANSWORLD PUBLISHERS
61–63 Uxbridge Road, London W5 5SA
Random House Group Company
www.transworldbooks.co.uk

First published in the United States
in 2013 by Clarkson Potter/Publishers
an imprint of the Crown Publishing Group
a division of Random House, Inc., New York

First published in Great Britain
in 2013 by Bantam Press
an imprint of Transworld Publishers

Some recipes and photographs in this book originally
appeared in Martha Stewart Living Omnimedia Publication.
Photography credits appear on page 375.
Book design by Deb Wood and Jessi Blackham.

A CIP catalogue record for this book is available from
the British Library.

ISBN 9780593072837

Addresses for Random House Group Ltd companies
outside the UK can be found at:
www.randomhouse.co.uk
The Random House Group Ltd Reg. No. 954009

The Random House Group Limited supports the Forest
Stewardship Council®(FSC®), the leading international
forest-certification organization. Our books carrying
the FSC label are printed on FSC®-certified paper. FSC
is the only forest-certification scheme supported by the
leading environmental organizations, including Green-
peace. Our paper procurement policy can be found at
www.randomhouse.co.uk/environment.

Printed and bound in Great Britain by Butler Tanner &
Dennis Ltd, Frome

10 9 8 7 6 5 4 3 2 1

To everyone who realizes that
a balanced diet relying more heavily on
vegetable than on animal can result
in a longer and healthier life

contents

foreword

I clearly remember the day when my daughter, Alexis, announced she would no longer be eating meat. She had just questioned the contents of a dinner I served her—a delicious small lamb chop, medium rare, the animal organically raised in our own backyard. I fibbed, telling her it was a pork chop, not wanting her to be upset that the pet sheep, Plantagenet Palliser, had been butchered and served at our family table. She made an educated guess, was right in her calculation, and declared, "No more meat, maybe fish." She was twelve at the time.

My diet had no such abrupt refining, but a gradual trending toward less and less meat, even less and less fish, until now I rely so much on other sorts of protein, on many vegetables, most of them farm raised, and on fruits and pastas. My shift has been the result of many things—books like Jonathan Safran Foer's *Eating Animals*, films such as *Food, Inc.,* and my very own observations of factory farms, feed lots, fish farms, and the condition of the meats and fish sold in many of our supermarkets. My own backyard has become my personal experimental laboratory for growing, organically, most of the vegetables and fruits that I consume, and I have built a large greenhouse and cold frame where I can now grow most of what I need even in the colder months of the year. I raise my own laying hens for delicious eggs for me and my family and friends, and I keep bees for pollination as well as for honey. I am waiting to build a small dairy until I have enough time to milk and make butter and cheese.

Encouraged by so many friends and colleagues who have made the shift to a more vegetable-based diet, and by Alexis and the extraordinarily good meals she makes for herself and her two small children, my colleagues and I have now published this book of vegetarian recipes. With the hard work and intelligent approach of our industrious *Whole Living* magazine editors, and the wonderful creative cooks in the kitchens at *Martha Stewart Living, Meatless* offers a wide range of recipes that will tempt even the most diehard meat eaters to expand their cooking repertoires to include more vegetable-based meals. Our more frequent trips to the farmer's markets and organic sections of the grocery stores will be more productive if armed with a recipe or two from these pages. With a recipe such as French Lentils with Caramelized Celery Root and Parsley, for example, you will not pass by those knobby, weird celeriac roots ever again wondering, "What could I possibly make with one of those?" And why not eliminate the sausage topping for your homemade pizzas and add instead flavorful broccoli rabe or thin slices of delicious, nutritious butternut squash?

Each recipe is illustrated with a photograph that will tempt you to try combinations of grains, nuts, vegetables, and seasonings you may have never thought of. And each recipe proves, in both large and small ways, with bold or sophisticated or simple combinations of ingredients, that *Meatless* can be an exciting and healthy and beneficial addition to your shelf of must-have cookbooks, and that Mother's age-old directive "Eat your vegetables" is still a very "Good Thing"!

Martha Stewart

introduction

THIS COOKBOOK IS FOR EVERYONE: everyone who loves food, and everyone who would like to eat more vegetables and less meat. The recipes cover every season, every major world cuisine—every craving. The Black-Rice Stir-Fry (page 93) and the Kale, Apple, and Beet Salad (page 224) would be at home in the best vegetarian restaurants in the country. The Lighter Macaroni and Cheese (page 152) and the Beans-and-Greens Tacos with Goat Cheese (page 259) are comfort food at their healthiest and best. Yes, the book is called *Meatless*. But funnily enough, it's not about getting less, but gaining more: more seasonal produce, more whole grains, more protein-rich beans, and more flavor.

There are many reasons to forgo meat and reach for plant foods, whether you dabble in such a diet occasionally (the Meatless Monday trend is growing rapidly) or you're a vegetarian every day of the week. Foremost among them, for many of us, are the health benefits that accrue with such a diet; the evidence that eating less meat protects against heart disease, cancer, and several other diseases is more and more compelling. And for all the dietary confusion we face, nutritionists have yet to say a bad word about vegetables. For some of us, it comes down to ethical concerns about animal welfare and the deplorable aspects of factory farming. For others, it's a matter of the environment: Raising animals for food on a large scale has involved the wholesale clearing of rain forests and the profligate consumption of water; it also continues to be a major contributor to greenhouse gases. For many, the decision to forgo meat is a combination of all of the reasons above.

And yet, when we sit down to eat, those reasons fade into the background. Any diet that's worth keeping has to make sense to our taste buds, not just our heads. The plate is the place to celebrate plant foods in all their delicious glory—their colors, flavors, textures, and versatility. (For identification, we've included the icons ❶ for "vegan," ❷ for "gluten-free," and ❸ for "special diet"—no dairy, wheat, soy, or nuts.) This cookbook is designed to provide page after page of options and inspiration for creating and enjoying meatless dishes. I'm so happy you're here to join me at the table.

ALANNA STANG
Editor in Chief, *Whole Living*

PROTEIN POWERHOUSES

One of the biggest concerns people have about going meatless is how to get enough protein from a plant-based diet. Yet there are plenty of protein-rich sources besides meat. Some foods—such as eggs, dairy, soy, quinoa, and buckwheat—contain complete proteins made up of the nine essential amino acids; most plant-based foods contain only some amino acids. However, contrary to what you may have heard, you don't need to worry about pairing certain foods at every meal to make complete proteins; just be sure to eat a variety of grains, legumes, fruits, and vegetables throughout the day. A good rule of thumb is to aim for half a gram of protein for each pound of body weight, or about 65 grams a day for a 130-pound woman.

PROTEIN	GRAMS PER SERVING	PROTEIN	GRAMS PER SERVING
Tempeh (4 ounces)	41 g	**Low-fat (1%) milk** (1 cup)	8 g
Seitan (3 ounces)	31 g	**Soy milk** (1 cup)	8 g
Lentils (1 cup cooked)	18 g	**Egg** (1 large, cooked)	7.5 g
Black beans (1 cup cooked)	15 g	**Cheddar cheese** (1 ounce)	7 g
Chickpeas (1 cup cooked)	12 g	**Wheat bread** (2 slices)	7 g
Edamame (½ cup cooked)	11 g	**Almonds** (1 ounce)	6 g
Tofu (4 ounces)	10 g	**Yogurt** (6 ounces)	6 g
Green peas (1 cup cooked)	9 g	**Bulgur** (1 cup cooked)	5.5 g
Quinoa (1 cup cooked)	8 g	**Spinach** (1 cup cooked)	5 g
Peanut butter (2 tablespoons)	8 g	**Broccoli** (1 cup cooked)	4 g

small plates to mix and match

Stuffed Marinated Hot Red Cherry Peppers

It's hard to resist the combination of melted cheese and tender pepper, but this recipe ups the ante with two flavor-boosting steps: a sprig of marjoram is tucked inside each pepper, and the peppers are marinated in a garlicky vinaigrette before baking. **MAKES 14**

14 hot red cherry peppers, seeds and cores removed, tops reserved

4 ounces Pecorino or provolone, cut into ¼-inch cubes

14 small sprigs fresh marjoram, plus more for garnish

¼ cup extra-virgin olive oil

2 tablespoons red-wine vinegar

1 garlic clove, minced

Coarse salt and freshly ground pepper

1 Dividing evenly, stuff each pepper with cheese and a sprig of marjoram. Arrange stuffed peppers and pepper tops in a glass loaf pan.

2 Whisk together olive oil, vinegar, and garlic in a small bowl; season with salt and pepper. Drizzle over peppers. Let marinate at room temperature 1 hour.

3 Preheat oven to 400°F. Place tops on peppers. Bake until cheese has melted and peppers are tender, 12 to 15 minutes. Let cool slightly before serving, garnished with more marjoram.

G Per serving: 141 calories, 12.32 g fat (3.89 g saturated fat), 11.18 mg cholesterol, 2.63 g carbohydrates, 4.21 g protein, 0.08 g fiber

Mediterranean Chickpea Salad

In this vibrant salad, chickpeas are tossed with fresh herbs and a colorful mix of finely chopped vegetables. **SERVES 6**

1 garlic clove, minced
Coarse salt

16 whole black peppercorns, crushed

3 tablespoons sherry vinegar

2 tablespoons extra-virgin olive oil

¾ teaspoon dried oregano

3 cups cooked chickpeas (see page 365), drained and rinsed

2 cups (8 ounces) cherry tomatoes, halved

½ English cucumber, peeled and cut into ½-inch dice

½ green bell pepper, ribs and seeds removed, cut into ½-inch dice (1 cup)

2 carrots, peeled and cut into ½-inch dice

3 scallions, trimmed and sliced ½ inch thick

3 tablespoons coarsely chopped fresh flat-leaf parsley leaves

2 tablespoons torn basil leaves, plus more for garnish

1 On a cutting board, press flat side of a chef's knife back and forth across garlic and ½ teaspoon salt to make a paste. Transfer to a large bowl, and whisk in crushed peppercorns, vinegar, olive oil, and oregano.

2 Add chickpeas, and toss to coat with dressing. Let stand 1 hour, stirring once or twice. Add tomatoes, cucumber, bell pepper, carrots, scallions, parsley, and torn basil. Toss to combine and serve garnished with whole basil leaves.

V G S Per serving: 196 calories, 6 g fat (1 g saturated fat), 0 mg cholesterol, 27 g carbohydrates, 8 g protein, 8 g fiber

Tortilla Española

This potato, onion, and egg omelet is the national dish of Spain—and a tapas-bar favorite. Small cubes or wedges are wonderful as part of a small-plates meal, as shown on page 12. **SERVES 8**

½ cup extra-virgin olive oil

4 saffron strands

2 large baking potatoes, peeled and thinly sliced

1 red onion, thinly sliced

5 garlic cloves, finely chopped

Coarse salt and freshly ground pepper

5 large eggs

½ cup coarsely chopped fresh flat-leaf parsley, plus more for garnish

1 tablespoon fresh thyme leaves (optional)

1 Preheat oven to 400°F. Heat olive oil and saffron in an ovenproof 8-inch skillet over medium. Add potatoes, onion, and garlic, and stir well. Press into an even layer with a spatula. Reduce heat to medium-low, cover, and cook 10 minutes. Stir potato mixture, season with salt and pepper, and press again. Cover, and cook 10 minutes. Transfer to a colander set over a bowl, and let drain, reserving oil. Wipe pan clean with paper towels.

2 In a medium bowl, whisk together eggs, parsley, and thyme (if using). Season with salt and pepper. Stir in potato mixture. Heat 2 tablespoons reserved oil in same skillet over medium. Pour in egg mixture, and gently press into an even layer. Reduce heat to medium-low. Cook, uncovered, 2 minutes.

3 Transfer skillet to oven and bake until eggs are set, about 5 minutes. To unmold, run a flexible spatula around edge of skillet; invert onto a serving plate (or serve directly from pan). Serve warm or at room temperature, garnished with more parsley.

G Per serving: 249 calories, 17 g fat (3 g saturated fat), 132 mg cholesterol, 18 g carbohydrates, 6 g protein, 2 g fiber

Lentil and Cashew Hummus

Making hummus from scratch means you can tinker with the basic formula to create something you just can't find in a store. Here, lentils and cashew butter replace chickpeas and tahini; for the best flavor, buy cashew butter that is freshly ground at a natural-foods market. **MAKES 2½ CUPS**

8 cups water

1 cup brown or green lentils, picked over and rinsed

¼ cup cashew butter

¼ cup plus 2 tablespoons fresh lemon juice (from 3 to 4 lemons)

½ teaspoon minced garlic

½ teaspoon hot sauce

Coarse salt

3 teaspoons extra-virgin olive oil

Fresh flat-leaf parsley leaves, for garnish

4 pocketless whole-wheat pitas, toasted or grilled and cut into wedges

1 Bring the water to a boil in a medium saucepan. Add lentils, reduce heat, and gently simmer until lentils are tender, about 30 minutes. Drain lentils, and let cool completely. (Lentils can be made 1 day ahead and refrigerated in an airtight container.)

2 Process cashew butter, lemon juice, garlic, hot sauce, and 1 teaspoon salt in a food processor until combined. Add lentils, and process until smooth, about 2 minutes. With motor running, add 2 teaspoons olive oil, and process until incorporated. Transfer to a bowl, and chill if desired up to 3 days, covered. Drizzle with remaining teaspoon oil, garnish with parsley, and serve with pitas.

V Per serving (¼ cup plus 1 tablespoon): 288 calories, 8 g fat (2 g saturated fat), 0 mg cholesterol, 43 g carbohydrates, 15 g protein, 7 g fiber

Charred Eggplant Dip

The smoky flavors of this dip get stronger—and better—after sitting in the refrigerator for a couple of days. Serve it with radishes, wax beans, or carrots, or in a sandwich with arugula, mozzarella, and roasted peppers. **MAKES 2 CUPS**

2 small eggplants

1 garlic clove, minced

1 to 2 tablespoons fresh lemon juice

Pinch of crushed red pepper flakes

Coarse salt

Extra-virgin olive oil, for drizzling

1 Heat broiler, with rack 6 inches from the heat source. Prick eggplants all over with a fork. Broil on a rimmed baking sheet, turning occasionally, until eggplants are soft and charred, about 20 minutes. When cool, remove and discard skin and stems and mash flesh.

2 Stir in garlic, lemon juice, and red pepper flakes; season with salt. Drizzle with olive oil before serving.

V G S Per serving (¼ cup plus 1 tablespoon): 65 calories, 3 g fat (0 g saturated fat), 0 mg cholesterol, 11 g carbohydrates, 2 g protein, 6 g fiber

Smashed Chickpea, Basil, and Radish Dip

Think of this dip as a crunchier hummus: the chickpeas are mashed in a bowl, rather than pureed, and then mixed with chopped radishes. **MAKES 3 CUPS**

- 3 cups cooked chickpeas (see page 365), drained and rinsed (reserve ⅓ cup liquid)
- 2 tablespoons extra-virgin olive oil
  Coarse salt and freshly ground pepper
- ½ cup fresh basil leaves, coarsely chopped
- 8 radishes, coarsley chopped
- 1 small garlic clove, minced
- ¼ cup fresh lemon juice (from 2 to 3 lemons)
- 9 whole-wheat pitas, split, toasted or grilled, and cut into quarters

1 Using a fork, lightly mash chickpeas, olive oil, 1 teaspoon salt, and ¾ teaspoon pepper in a bowl until creamy but still chunky.

2 Stir in basil, radishes, garlic, and lemon juice; season with more salt and pepper, as desired. Stir in reserved chickpea liquid, 1 tablespoon at a time, until dip holds together. Cover and refrigerate for at least 30 minutes (or up to 3 days, adding basil just before serving). Serve with pita chips.

V Per serving (¼ cup dip with 6 pita chips): 220 calories, 4 g fat (1 g saturated fat), 0 mg cholesterol, 39 g carbohydrates, 9 g protein, 6 g fiber

Fresh Pea Hummus

Green peas are a good source of protein: one cup has more protein than a large egg. They are naturally sweet, especially when just released from their shells. Fresh peas form the base of this dip, flavored with cilantro, lemon juice, and cumin. Thawed frozen peas can be used in place of fresh. **MAKES 1¼ CUPS**

- 1 cup fresh shelled peas
  Coarse salt
- ¼ cup fresh cilantro (leaves and stems)
- 2 tablespoons tahini
- 2 tablespoons fresh lemon juice
- 1 small garlic clove, minced
- ⅛ teaspoon ground cumin
  Whole-grain crackers, for serving

1 Cook peas in a pot of boiling salted water until tender, about 2 minutes. Drain; run under cold water to stop the cooking.

2 Pulse peas, cilantro, tahini, lemon juice, garlic, and cumin in food processor until smooth, 30 to 40 seconds. Season with salt and serve with crackers.

V **S** Per serving (¼ cup plus 1 tablespoon): 74 calories, 4 g fat (1 g saturated fat), 0 mg cholesterol, 7 g carbohydrates, 3 g protein, 2 g fiber

Roasted Sweet Potato Salsa

Roasted diced sweet potatoes turn ordinary salsa into a more substantial dip. Spoon it onto crackers or chips, use it as a filling for tacos or omelets, or serve it atop rice and beans. **MAKES 4 CUPS**

1 large sweet potato (1 pound), peeled and cut into small dice

1 red onion, cut into small dice

1 tablespoon extra-virgin olive oil

1 tomato, seeds removed, cut into small dice

1 ripe, firm avocado, halved, pitted, peeled, and cut into small dice

2 tablespoons chopped fresh cilantro leaves

¼ cup fresh lime juice (from 2 to 3 limes)

Coarse salt

1 Preheat oven to 450°F. On a rimmed baking sheet, toss together sweet potato, onion, and olive oil. Spread in an even layer and roast until sweet potato is tender and browned in spots, tossing once or twice, about 20 minutes.

2 Transfer to a large bowl and let cool completely. Add tomato, avocado, cilantro, and lime juice. Season with salt, toss to combine, and serve.

V G S Per serving (¼ cup): 55 calories, 3 g fat (0 g saturated fat), 0 mg cholesterol, 8 g carbohydrates, 1 g protein, 2 g fiber

Roasted Potatoes with Romesco Sauce

Romesco, from the Catalonia region of Spain, is a versatile all-purpose sauce. Versions abound, some made with fresh tomatoes, others (like the one here) with red peppers. All are thickened with nuts (typically almonds) and sometimes bread. Romesco is delicious as an accompaniment for roasted potatoes or other vegetables. Or try it spread on thick slices of toasted rustic bread with grilled leeks or ramps. **SERVES 4**

½ cup blanched almonds, toasted (see page 363)

1 small garlic clove

2 red bell peppers, roasted (see page 364)

⅛ teaspoon smoked hot paprika

¼ cup loosely packed fresh mint leaves

1 teaspoon sherry vinegar or red-wine vinegar

Coarse salt

1 tablespoon plus 1½ teaspoons extra-virgin olive oil

1 pound small red, yellow, or purple potatoes, larger ones cut in half

1. Preheat oven to 375°F. In a food processor, combine almonds, garlic, roasted red peppers, paprika, mint, vinegar, and ¾ teaspoon salt. Process to a coarse paste, about 1 minute. With machine running, add 1 tablespoon olive oil in a slow, steady stream until sauce is smooth. Transfer sauce to a small bowl.

2. Arrange potatoes on a rimmed baking sheet, drizzle with remaining 1½ teaspoons oil, and season with salt. Toss to combine, and roast until skins are slightly crisp and potatoes are tender, shaking pan halfway through to turn potatoes, 20 to 30 minutes. Serve potatoes with romesco sauce on the side.

V G Per serving: 218 calories, 16 g fat (1.5 g saturated fat), 0 mg cholesterol, 15 g carbohydrates, 7 g protein, 7 g fiber

Summer Rolls with Carrot-Ginger Dipping Sauce

Rice-paper wrappers are easy to work with: simply soak in hot water for a few seconds until pliable, then wrap around crisp vegetables—beet, carrot, cucumber, bell pepper, and daikon are used here—for no-cook summer rolls. The pureed carrot-ginger dipping sauce can double as a salad dressing for mixed baby lettuces. Look for rice-paper wrappers in the Asian-pantry section of supermarkets. **MAKES 6**

FOR THE ROLLS

- 6 rice-paper wrappers (8-inch size)
- 2 cups (½ ounce) radish or alfalfa sprouts
- 1 red beet, scrubbed, trimmed, and very thinly sliced crosswise
- 1 carrot, peeled and cut into matchsticks
- 1 Kirby cucumber, cut into matchsticks
- 1 red bell pepper, ribs and seeds removed, cut into matchsticks
- ¾ cup coarsely grated daikon radish

FOR THE SAUCE

- 3 carrots, peeled and coarsely chopped
- 1 small shallot, quartered
- 2 tablespoons coarsely grated peeled fresh ginger
- ¼ cup rice vinegar (unseasoned)
- 2 tablespoons low-sodium soy sauce
- ¼ teaspoon toasted-sesame oil

  Pinch each of coarse salt and freshly ground pepper
- ¼ cup canola or safflower oil
- ¼ cup water

1 Make the rolls: Soak 1 rice-paper wrapper in a large bowl of hot water just until pliable. Transfer to a work surface and smooth to make flat. Place one-sixth of the sprouts, beet slices, carrot, cucumber, bell pepper, and daikon on bottom third of wrapper, leaving a 1½-inch border. Fold bottom of paper over fillings, tuck in sides, and roll up tightly to enclose. Repeat with remaining wrappers and filling ingredients to make 5 more rolls.

2 Make the sauce: Puree carrots, shallot, ginger, vinegar, soy sauce, sesame oil, salt, and pepper in a food processor until smooth. With machine running, add canola or safflower oil and then water through the feed tube in a slow, steady stream until smooth. Serve sauce with summer rolls.

V G Per serving: 185 calories, 10 g fat (1 g saturated fat), 0 mg cholesterol, 19 g carbohydrates, 4 g protein, 3 g fiber

Kale and Red Cabbage Slaw

This tangy kale-and-cabbage slaw gets ample protein (and healthy fats) from a trio of seeds: sunflower, pumpkin, and hemp. The last tops the list of nuts and seeds as a source of high-quality (complete) protein. Hemp seeds are available whole or hulled at health-food stores, and either type can be used in this recipe. **SERVES 4**

1 tablespoon Dijon mustard

1 teaspoon apple cider vinegar

1 tablespoon extra-virgin olive oil

Coarse salt and freshly ground pepper

3 cups mixed finely shredded kale and red cabbage

1 carrot, peeled and julienned

¼ cup fresh flat-leaf parsley leaves

2 tablespoons diced red onion

2 tablespoons hulled sunflower seeds

2 tablespoons pepitas (hulled pumpkin seeds)

2 tablespoons hemp seeds

1 In a small bowl, whisk together mustard, vinegar, and olive oil; season with salt and pepper.

2 In another bowl, combine kale and cabbage, carrot, parsley, onion, and all seeds. Drizzle with dressing and season with salt and pepper. Toss to coat. Serve.

V G S Per serving: 111 calories, 7 g fat (1 g saturated fat), 0 mg cholesterol, 9.55 g carbohydrates, 5 g protein, 3 g fiber

Zucchini "Pasta" with Tomatoes and Walnuts

Not only is this vibrant dish gluten-free, it also requires no cooking. Thin strips of zucchini stand in for pasta strands, and are topped with tomatoes, basil, and chopped walnuts. With so few ingredients, the quality of each one is crucial; use peak-of-season squash and a top-quality extra-virgin olive oil. **SERVES 2**

8   ounces cherry tomatoes, halved

1   garlic clove, thinly sliced

¼   cup chopped walnuts

2   tablespoons torn fresh basil leaves, plus whole leaves for garnish

2   tablespoons extra-virgin olive oil, plus more for drizzling

Sea salt

1   zucchini

1   In a medium bowl, combine tomatoes, garlic, walnuts, torn basil, and 2 tablespoons olive oil. Season with salt. Let stand 20 minutes.

2   Thinly slice zucchini lengthwise, then cut slices into ¼-inch-wide strips. Add to tomato mixture and toss to combine. Garnish with whole basil leaves, and serve.

V G Per serving: 255 calories, 24 g fat (3 g saturated fat), 0 mg cholesterol, 10 g carbohydrates, 5 g protein, 3 g fiber

Roasted Beets and Edamame with Arugula

Golden beets lend the dish a beautiful color, but any variety will do. Similarly, you can substitute ordinary arugula if you can't find baby arugula. **SERVES 4**

3 medium golden beets

2 tablespoons plus
   1 teaspoon olive oil,
   plus more for drizzling

1 cup frozen shelled
   edamame, thawed

   Coarse salt and freshly
   ground pepper

1 tablespoon red-wine
   vinegar

3 cups baby arugula

½ cup fresh basil leaves

1 Preheat oven to 425°F. Drizzle beets with olive oil; wrap in parchment, then in foil. Roast on a rimmed baking sheet until tender, about 1 hour. When just cool enough to handle, rub off skins, then slice beets thin.

2 Meanwhile, on another rimmed baking sheet, toss edamame with 1 teaspoon oil; season with salt and pepper. Roast, tossing halfway through, until golden, 20 to 25 minutes. Let cool slightly.

3 In a small bowl, whisk together vinegar and remaining 2 tablespoons olive oil. In a medium bowl, combine arugula, basil, beets, and edamame. Toss with dressing, season with salt and pepper, and serve.

V G S Per serving: 154 calories, 9 g fat (1 g saturated fat), 0 mg cholesterol, 10.32 g carbohydrates, 7 g protein, 5 g fiber

Avocado Salad with Bell Pepper and Tomatoes

Avocado shells make handy vessels for a bright salad made with the scooped-out flesh. Lime juice, garlic, and a pinch of cayenne flavor the dressing. The salad can also be served as a topping for quesadillas or as a fresh filling for tacos. **SERVES 1**

1 teaspoon extra-virgin olive oil

Juice of ½ lime

1 small garlic clove, minced

Pinch of cayenne pepper

Coarse salt

1 firm, ripe avocado, halved and pitted

½ yellow bell pepper, ribs and seeds removed, diced

6 cherry tomatoes, halved

1 scallion, trimmed and thinly sliced

1 tablespoon chopped fresh cilantro leaves, plus whole leaves for garnish

1 In a small bowl, whisk together olive oil, lime juice, garlic, and cayenne. Season with salt.

2 Scoop out flesh from avocado halves, reserving shells, and chop. Transfer to a bowl and add bell pepper, tomatoes, scallion, and chopped cilantro.

3 Drizzle with dressing and season with salt. Gently stir to combine. Spoon mixture into reserved shells. Garnish with whole cilantro leaves and serve immediately.

V G S Per serving: 424 calories, 34.63 g fat (5 g saturated fat), 0 mg cholesterol, 31.25 g carbohydrates, 6.6 g protein, 16.36 g fiber

Potato and Leek Galette with Watercress

Like other potato dishes, galettes partner well with a variety of flavors, and they are sized (and shaped) just right for sharing. This one is topped with lightly dressed watercress; arugula, chicory, and mâche are other good greens. **SERVES 8**

1 large russet potato, peeled and grated (about 1½ cups)

1 small leek, white and pale-green parts only, thinly sliced crosswise, washed well and drained

3 tablespoons all-purpose flour

Pinch of freshly grated nutmeg

Coarse salt and freshly ground pepper

2 tablespoons plus 1½ teaspoons olive oil

1 cup watercress, trimmed

½ teaspoon fresh lemon juice

1 Place grated potato in a bowl of cold water, and let soak 10 minutes. Drain well in a salad spinner or squeeze in a clean kitchen towel to remove excess water. Combine potato, leek, flour, nutmeg, ¾ teaspoon salt, and ¼ teaspoon pepper.

2 Heat 2 tablespoons olive oil in a large nonstick skillet over medium. Scatter potato mixture in skillet, and gently press into an even layer with a spatula. Cook until golden on bottom, about 6 minutes. Run a flexible spatula around edge of skillet. Invert galette onto a plate, then return to skillet. Raise heat to medium-high. Cook until other side is golden, 4 to 5 minutes.

3 Invert galette onto plate. In a bowl, toss watercress with lemon juice and remaining 1½ teaspoons oil, and place on top of galette. Slice into 8 wedges and serve immediately.

V Per serving: 93 calories, 4.5 g fat (.64 g saturated fat), 0 mg cholesterol, 12 g carbohydrates, 1.5 g protein, 1 g fiber

Sweet Potatoes with Coconut, Pomegranate, and Lime

Roasted sweet potatoes go from simple to sublime with exceptional toppings. This one has Middle Eastern flavors: coconut (milk and flakes), pomegranate seeds, cilantro, and lime juice. To extract the pomegranate seeds, split a fruit into quarters, and peel seeds from membrane. **SERVES 4**

4 medium sweet potatoes, scrubbed

¼ cup unsweetened coconut flakes

¼ cup light coconut milk

2 tablespoons chopped fresh cilantro leaves, plus sprigs for garnish

1 cup pomegranate seeds

Coarse salt

Lime wedges, for serving

1 Preheat oven to 400°F. Prick sweet potatoes all over with a fork. Arrange on a rimmed baking sheet and roast until tender, about 45 minutes. Let cool slightly.

2 Meanwhile, spread coconut flakes on another rimmed baking sheet and toast until lightly browned, tossing once or twice, about 5 minutes.

3 Slice the top of each sweet potato to open and mash the interior with a fork. Divide coconut milk, coconut flakes, chopped cilantro, and pomegranate seeds evenly among sweet potatoes. Season each with salt. Garnish with sprigs of cilantro and serve with lime wedges for squeezing over each.

V G S Per serving: 272 calories, 9 g fat (8 g saturated fat), 0 mg cholesterol, 44 g carbohydrates, 5 g protein, 9 g fiber

Baked Artichokes with Bread Crumbs

This simple Italian preparation—which also works well as a side dish—is one of the easiest ways to enjoy fresh artichokes; when baked under layers of cheese and bread crumbs, the artichokes become delectably tender. **SERVES 4**

1 cup fresh bread crumbs, toasted (see page 363)

1 tablespoon extra-virgin olive oil

1 tablespoon sliced fresh chives (½-inch lengths)

½ teaspoon finely grated lemon zest

1 garlic clove, minced

½ cup grated Gruyère cheese

Coarse salt and freshly ground pepper

2 artichokes

1 Preheat oven to 400°F. In a small bowl, combine bread crumbs, olive oil, chives, lemon zest, garlic, and cheese. Season with salt and pepper.

2 With a sharp knife, cut off the top quarter of each artichoke, then remove the small leaves from the bottom. Cut artichoke in half lengthwise. Use a melon baller or small spoon to remove choke.

3 Season artichokes with salt. Divide the bread-crumb mixture evenly among the 4 artichoke halves, packing it into the cavities.

4 Place artichokes in a baking dish just large enough to hold them. Add about ½ inch of water, and cover tightly with parchment, then foil.

5 Bake until the artichokes are tender and the bread crumbs are golden brown, about 1 hour. Serve immediately.

Per serving: 232 calories, 9.42 g fat (3.4 g saturated fat), 14.85 mg cholesterol, 28.07 g carbohydrates, 10.31 g protein, 5.63 g fiber

White Bean and Sage Patties with Roasted Tomatoes

Just a handful of ingredients—cooked beans, shallot, carrot, sage, and cornmeal (not flour)—make up these golden patties, which are accompanied by a deeply flavorful roasted-tomato sauce. Depending on the number of people you are serving, you may want to make multiple batches; the patties and sauce have a tendency to quickly disappear. **MAKES 12**

2¼ cups cooked white beans (see page 365)

½ shallot, finely chopped

1 small carrot, finely grated

⅓ cup yellow cornmeal

1 teaspoon chopped fresh sage leaves

Coarse salt and freshly ground pepper

¼ cup olive oil

Roasted Tomato Sauce (page 368), for serving

1 Drain beans, reserving liquid. Transfer beans to a bowl and mash. Stir in shallot, carrot, cornmeal, and sage. Season with salt and pepper. If mixture is too dry, add 1 to 2 tablespoons reserved liquid.

2 Heat a large skillet over medium-high. Add 2 tablespoons olive oil. Form bean mixture into 12 patties (about 2½ inches diameter each) and sauté in batches until golden brown and crisp, 2 to 3 minutes per side. Repeat with remaining oil and patties. Season patties with salt and serve with sauce.

V G S Per serving (2 patties): 228 calories, 10 g fat (1 g saturated fat), 0 mg cholesterol, 29 g carbohydrates, 9 g protein, 7 g fiber

Artichoke Hearts Roman Style

In Rome, artichokes are traditionally braised in a flavorful herb mixture that includes a native wild mint. Stateside varieties of fresh mint will work just fine in this recipe. Fresh artichokes are a must; see page 364 for how to extract the hearts. **SERVES 4**

½ cup plus 2 tablespoons fresh flat-leaf parsley leaves, finely chopped

½ cup plus 2 tablespoons fresh mint leaves, finely chopped

2 garlic cloves, minced

½ cup plus 1 tablespoon extra-virgin olive oil

Coarse salt and freshly ground pepper

4 fresh artichoke hearts

1. In a bowl, combine ½ cup parsley, ½ cup mint, the garlic, and 1 tablespoon olive oil. Season with salt and pepper.

2. Rub artichoke hearts inside and out with herb mixture. Place them stem side up in a medium pot. Add remaining ½ cup oil and enough water to come halfway up the sides of the artichoke hearts. Bring to a boil over high heat. Reduce heat to low, cover, and simmer until artichokes are tender, about 20 minutes. Remove pot from heat and add remaining herbs. Cool artichokes completely in the cooking liquid.

3. Divide artichoke hearts among 4 plates, and serve at room temperature with some of the cooking liquid spooned over the top.

Ⓥ Ⓖ Ⓢ Per serving: 222 calories, 16.05 g fat (2.28 g saturated fat), 0 mg cholesterol, 17.87 g carbohydrates, 5.56 g protein, 9.08 g fiber

Gigante Beans with Feta and Greens

Dandelion greens give this Greek stew the most authentic flavor, but you could substitute blanched Swiss chard or chicory. In Greece the beans are often served with a selection of small plates; see page 372 for a suggested menu. **SERVES 4**

- 2 tablespoons plus 1 teaspoon olive oil
- 2 cups finely chopped onions
- 2 garlic cloves, thinly sliced
- 2 tablespoons tomato paste
- 8 ounces dried gigante beans, soaked and drained (see page 365)
- 1 pound tomatoes, blanched and peeled (see page 364), and finely chopped
- 1 bunch dandelion greens, tough stems trimmed, cut into 3-inch pieces
- 1 tablespoon red-wine vinegar

  Coarse salt
- ½ cup crumbled feta
- 3 tablespoons coarsely chopped fresh dill

1 Heat 1 tablespoon olive oil in a medium pot over medium. Cook onion until soft, stirring frequently, 8 to 10 minutes. Add garlic and tomato paste. Cook, stirring, until fragrant, 2 to 3 minutes.

2 Add beans, tomatoes, and 4½ cups water and bring to a boil. Reduce heat to a bare simmer, partially cover, and cook until beans are tender, about 45 minutes.

3 Meanwhile, prepare an ice-water bath. Blanch dandelion greens in a pot of boiling water until tender and no longer bitter, about 4 minutes. Transfer to ice bath using a slotted spoon.

4 Once beans are tender, add vinegar and 1 teaspoon salt. Drain dandelion greens, and add to beans. Cook, stirring, until heated through. To serve, divide beans and greens among 4 bowls, top with feta and dill, and drizzle with remaining oil.

G Per serving: 293 calories, 10 g fat (3 g saturated fat), 6 mg cholesterol, 50 g carbohydrates, 19 g protein, 24 g fiber

Grilled Polenta and Balsamic Mushrooms

The trick to grilling polenta is to know when to flip it: wait until it can be lifted from the grates cleanly with a metal spatula, without tearing the crisp surface. **SERVES 4**

6 portobello mushrooms (about 1 pound), stems and caps separated, caps halved if very large

2 garlic cloves, coarsely chopped

2 tablespoons coarsely chopped fresh flat-leaf parsley

1 teaspoon coarsely chopped fresh thyme

⅓ cup balsamic vinegar

¼ cup plus 1 tablespoon extra-virgin olive oil, plus more for brushing

Coarse salt and freshly ground pepper

½ cup vegetable stock, preferably homemade (see page 364)

Basic polenta (firm; see page 366), cut into 12 pieces

2 cups arugula (2 ounces), washed and drained

Shaved Parmigiano-Reggiano, for garnish

1. Combine mushrooms, garlic, herbs, vinegar, and ¼ cup olive oil in a large bowl; season with salt and pepper and toss. Let stand at room temperature, tossing occasionally, 1 hour.

2. Transfer mushrooms to a plate. Pour marinade and stock into a small saucepan, and bring to a boil. Reduce heat, and simmer until reduced by half, about 10 minutes. Stir in remaining tablespoon oil, and remove from heat.

3. Heat grill to medium-high (see page 364). Lightly brush top and bottom of polenta pieces with oil, and place in center of grill. Cook, flipping once, until polenta is browned in spots and crisp, 6 to 8 minutes per side. Meanwhile, place mushrooms on cooler part of grill and cook, turning frequently to avoid burning, until tender, about 10 minutes.

4. Place arugula on a platter, and top with polenta and mushrooms. Drizzle with about half the sauce. Garnish with cheese and serve with extra sauce on the side.

G Per serving: 408 calories, 23.86 g fat (4.2 g saturated fat), 6.24 mg cholesterol, 36.68 g carbohydrates, 9.25 g protein, 4.08 g fiber

Stuffed Acorn Squash with Quinoa and Pistachios

A stuffing of quinoa, pistachios, and feta cheese elevates acorn squash from side dish to main course. For a vegan version, omit the feta and season the stuffing with one to two tablespoons nutritional yeast for a cheese flavor. Serve the squash with the kale slaw on page 31 or with sautéed greens, such as Swiss chard (see page 347) or broccolini (see page 335). **SERVES 8**

4 small acorn squash, halved, seeds removed

¼ cup olive oil

Coarse salt and freshly ground black pepper

2 cups water

1 cup quinoa, rinsed and drained

½ cup chopped fresh flat-leaf parsley leaves

½ cup feta cheese, crumbled

½ cup roasted, salted pistachios, chopped

2 teaspoons red-wine vinegar

Pinch of crushed red pepper flakes

1 Preheat oven to 425°F. Brush cut sides of squash halves with 2 tablespoons olive oil and season with salt and black pepper. Roast cut side down on 2 baking sheets until tender and caramelized, 15 to 20 minutes.

2 Meanwhile, bring the water and quinoa to a boil in a small pot. Stir once, cover, and reduce heat to a simmer. Cook until quinoa is tender but still chewy and has absorbed all the liquid, about 15 minutes. Fluff quinoa with a fork.

3 In a large bowl, combine quinoa, parsley, feta, pistachios, remaining 2 tablespoons oil, and vinegar. Season with salt and red pepper flakes. Divide filling among squash and serve.

G Per serving: 300 calories, 14 g fat (3 g saturated fat), 8 mg cholesterol, 40 g carbohydrates, 8 g protein, 5 g fiber

Omelet with Asparagus, Greens, and Pecorino

An oversize omelet easily feeds more than one person when filled with an abundance of asparagus, arugula, and cheese and sliced into wedges. **SERVES 4**

½ bunch asparagus, tough ends trimmed, cut into 1-inch pieces

   Coarse salt and freshly ground pepper

1 tablespoon extra-virgin olive oil

8 large eggs

2 tablespoons grated Pecorino Romano

¾ cup baby arugula

1 Prepare an ice-water bath. Blanch asparagus in a pot of boiling salted water until bright green and just tender, about 2 minutes. Transfer to the ice bath to cool, then drain.

2 Heat a large skillet over medium-low. Add olive oil and swirl to coat. Whisk eggs in a bowl and season with salt and pepper. Pour into pan and cook until omelet is just set, tilting pan and lifting up sides of set egg with a spatula to allow uncooked egg to run underneath, 7 to 8 minutes.

3 Top half of omelet with Pecorino Romano, asparagus, and arugula. Flip other half over top and cook until cheese melts, about 30 seconds more. Cut into wedges to serve.

Ⓖ Per serving: 203 calories, 14 g fat (4 g saturated fat), 425 mg cholesterol, 3 g carbohydrates, 15 g protein, 1 g fiber

VERSATILE VEGETARIAN:
BRUSCHETTA

Originally devised as a way to use stale bread, bruschetta can support a range of toppings. The tomato-and-balsamic version below is a good place to start; turn the page for more ideas. Serve bruschetta as part of a selection of small plates (see page 372), as a starter for a larger meal, or to accompany any manner of salads.

GRILL THE BREAD

RUB WITH GARLIC

DRIZZLE WITH OIL

TOMATO BRUSCHETTA MAKES 8

- 8 slices (¾ inch thick) rustic bread
- 1 head garlic, cut in half crosswise

  Extra-virgin olive oil

  Coarse salt and freshly ground black pepper
- 2 cups halved cherry or teardrop tomatoes (10 ounces)
- 2 teaspoons balsamic vinegar

  Pinch of crushed red pepper flakes

  Dill sprigs, for garnish

1. Heat grill (or grill pan) to medium (see page 364). Toast bread slices until golden brown, about 5 minutes per side. (Alternatively, broil bread about 1 minute per side.)

2. Remove toasts from grill, and immediately rub with cut side of the garlic head. (The warmth of the bread releases the garlic's aroma.)

3. On a cutting board or baking sheet, drizzle olive oil generously over toasts. Sprinkle with salt and black pepper. Cut slices in half.

4. Toss tomatoes with balsamic vinegar, a drizzle of oil, and red pepper flakes in a bowl. Season with salt and black pepper. Spoon onto toasts, and garnish with a few dill sprigs. Serve immediately.

V Per serving: 118 calories, 1.85 g fat (0.34 g saturated fat), 0 mg cholesterol, 21.27 g carbohydrates, 4.39 g protein, 1.32 g fiber

WILD MUSHROOMS
AND GARLIC

FAVA BEANS, MINT, AND
PECORINO ROMANO

LEMON AND GREEN-
OLIVE RELISH

CHARRED CARROTS
WITH GOAT CHEESE
AND PARSLEY

WILTED SUMMER GREENS
WITH GOAT CHEESE

FRESH RICOTTA WITH
LEMON, BASIL, AND HONEY

Wild Mushrooms and Garlic MAKES 8

Sauté 1½ pounds chopped fresh MUSHROOMS, such as chanterelle, porcini, or oyster, and 1 minced GARLIC clove and 1 tablespoon fresh THYME LEAVES in 2 tablespoons OLIVE OIL until mushrooms are golden and starting to release their juice. Season with coarse SALT and freshly ground PEPPER. Deglaze pan with ¼ cup dry WHITE WINE, scraping up any brown bits with a wooden spoon; season with more salt and pepper, as desired. (If using more than one type of mushroom, cook in batches, as their cooking times may vary.) Top toasts with mushrooms.

V Per serving: 101 calories, 4.18 g fat (0.63 g saturated fat), 0 mg cholesterol, 11.09 g carbohydrates, 3.74 g protein, 1.48 g fiber

Charred Carrots with Goat Cheese and Parsley MAKES 8

Preheat oven to 400°F. On a rimmed baking sheet, drizzle 1 pound CARROTS, peeled and chopped, with EXTRA-VIRGIN OLIVE OIL, and season with coarse SALT. Roast in a single layer until soft and charred, tossing occasionally, about 35 minutes. Toss together ¼ cup fresh flat-leaf PARSLEY leaves with 1 tablespoon each RED-WINE VINEGAR and EXTRA-VIRGIN OLIVE OIL. Mash carrots, and spread onto toasts; top with ⅓ cup crumbled GOAT CHEESE and the parsley mixture.

Per serving: 120 calories, 6.73 g fat (1.4 g saturated fat), 1.63 mg cholesterol, 12.78 g carbohydrates, 2.76 g protein, 2.54 g fiber

Wilted Summer Greens with Goat Cheese MAKES 8

Sauté 1 thinly sliced ONION in 1 tablespoon OLIVE OIL over medium heat until translucent, about 3 minutes. Add 1 pound mixed LEAFY SUMMER GREENS, such as spinach, arugula, and mizuna; cover and cook until wilted, about 1 minute. Uncover and cook until greens are tender, 1 to 2 minutes more; season with coarse SALT and freshly ground PEPPER. Let cool to room temperature; toss with ½ teaspoon SHERRY VINEGAR. Top toasts with ½ cup fresh GOAT CHEESE and greens mixture.

Per serving: 91 calories, 4.07 g fat (1.44 g saturated fat), 3.26 mg cholesterol, 10.25 g carbohydrates, 4.61 g protein, 2.35 g fiber

Fava Beans, Mint, and Pecorino Romano MAKES 8

Toss 2½ cups blanched and peeled FAVA BEANS, drained and rinsed, with 2 tablespoons EXTRA-VIRGIN OLIVE OIL, 1½ teaspoons fresh LEMON JUICE, and ¼ cup chopped MINT leaves. Season with coarse SALT, freshly ground PEPPER, and a pinch of CRUSHED RED PEPPER FLAKES. Spoon onto toasts. Top with thin shavings of PECORINO ROMANO (2 ounces).

Per serving: 155 calories, 6.32 g fat (1.78 g saturated fat), 5 mg cholesterol, 18.21 g carbohydrates, 7.65 g protein, 3.9 g fiber

Lemon and Green-Olive Relish MAKES 8

Combine 1 cup chopped pitted GREEN OLIVES; 1 peeled, seeded, and chopped LEMON; 1 tablespoon minced RED ONION; 1 diced CELERY stalk; ¼ teaspoon SUGAR; 3 tablespoons EXTRA-VIRGIN OLIVE OIL; and 3 tablespoons chopped fresh flat-leaf PARSLEY leaves. Season with coarse SALT and freshly ground PEPPER. Spread onto toasts.

V Per serving: 117 calories, 8.6 g fat (1.23 g saturated fat), 0 mg cholesterol, 9.33 g carbohydrates, 1.93 g protein, 1.93 g fiber

Fresh Ricotta with Lemon, Basil, and Honey MAKES 8

Mix 8 ounces RICOTTA, preferably fresh, with 2 teaspoons finely grated LEMON ZEST, and spread onto toasts (do not rub with garlic or drizzle with oil). Add a few fresh BASIL leaves, and drizzle with a delicate HONEY, such as acacia.

Per serving: 153 calories, 4.28 g fat (2.48 g saturated fat), 14.46 mg cholesterol, 25.71 g carbohydrates, 4.84 g protein, 1.05 g fiber

stovetop suppers

Skillet Greens with Eggs and Mushrooms

Even when the refrigerator is practically bare, there are almost always at least a few eggs, the foundation for this fifteen-minute dinner. Sauté some mushrooms and a bunch of greens (such as kale) and then crack in the eggs. It's especially delicious served over soft polenta, or with toasted rustic bread. **SERVES 4**

FOR THE SAGE-CHILE BUTTER (OPTIONAL)

- 4 tablespoons (½ stick) unsalted butter
- 1 tablespoon small fresh sage leaves
- ¼ teaspoon crushed red pepper flakes

FOR THE EGGS AND GREENS

- 2 tablespoons olive oil
- 10 ounces white button or cremini mushrooms, thinly sliced

  Coarse salt
- 2 garlic cloves, thinly sliced
- 6 cups sliced trimmed cooking greens (¾-inch-wide ribbons)
- 2 tablespoons water
- 2 tablespoons unsalted butter
- 4 large eggs

  Shaved Parmigiano-Reggiano, for garnish

1. Make the sage-chile butter, if desired: Melt butter in a saucepan over medium. Cook sage and red pepper flakes until sage is crisp, about 3 minutes. Remove from heat.

2. Make the eggs and greens: Heat a large, heavy skillet (preferably cast iron) over high. Swirl in olive oil. Add mushrooms and season with salt; cook until golden and tender, stirring occasionally, 4 to 5 minutes. Reduce heat to medium. Stir in garlic, greens, and the water. Cook, stirring, until greens wilt. Add butter, and stir until melted.

3. Make 4 wells in greens. Crack 1 egg into each well. Season with salt. Cook undisturbed 4 minutes. Remove from heat; let stand until whites are set but yolks are still runny, about 4 minutes more. Drizzle with sage-chile butter, if using, garnish with cheese, and serve.

G Per serving: 376 calories, 31.01 g fat (14.24 g saturated fat), 261.05 mg cholesterol, 14.22 g carbohydrates, 13.61 g protein, 2.5 g fiber

Greens and Herb Omelet

An omelet is the perfect meal, any time of day, needing only a simple salad as an accompaniment. **MAKES 1**

 1 tablespoon plus 1 teaspoon olive oil
 ½ onion, thinly sliced
     Coarse salt and freshly ground pepper
1½ cups chopped greens, such as spinach, kale, or Swiss chard (trimmed and washed)
 2 large whole eggs plus 1 large egg white
 1 to 2 tablespoons chopped fresh herbs, such as flat-leaf parsley, tarragon, or chives
 2 tablespoons crumbled feta or goat cheese

1 Heat 1 tablespoon olive oil in a nonstick skillet over medium-high. Sauté onion until soft, stirring often, about 5 minutes; season with salt and pepper. Stir in greens and cook until wilted, about 30 seconds more. Remove from pan. Whisk together whole eggs, white, and herbs in a bowl.

2 Heat remaining teaspoon oil in pan; add egg mixture. Reduce heat to medium. Cook, stirring eggs with a flexible spatula and shaking the pan over heat, until curds begin to form, about 1 minute. Continue cooking, pulling cooked egg from edge to center of pan with spatula, until omelet is just set, 15 to 30 seconds more.

3 Sprinkle greens mixture and cheese over half of the omelet, then gently fold over the other side, slide out of pan onto a plate, and serve.

Ⓖ Per serving: 594 calories, 49 g fat (15 g saturated fat), 449 mg cholesterol, 29 g protein, 10.54 g carbohydrates, 2.46 g fiber

Buddha Bowl

With whole grains, plant proteins, and vegetables, this is the ideal vegan one-bowl dish. It's more of a general formula than a hard-and-fast recipe, since you can swap out different ingredients for variety and to make use of whatever you have on hand. Choosing vegetables in a range of colors will ensure a balance of nutrients. And try adding dried seaweed—kombu, wakame, hijiki, or dulse—softened according to package instructions. **SERVES 1**

2 cups chopped or sliced vegetables, such as delicata squash, stemmed shiitake mushrooms, cauliflower florets, or small carrots (halved lengthwise)

½ cup cooked quinoa, millet, or brown rice (see page 371)

3 ounces tofu or ½ cup cooked beans (see page 365)

2 teaspoons sesame oil

Tamari soy sauce

Radish sprouts, for garnish (optional)

Chopped fresh herbs, for garnish (optional)

1 Set a steamer basket or colander in a saucepan filled with 2 inches water. Arrange vegetables in basket in an even layer. Cover and steam until vegetables are just tender, 2 to 4 minutes.

2 Layer the quinoa, tofu, and vegetables in a bowl. Sprinkle with the sesame oil and a splash of tamari. Garnish with sprouts or chopped fresh herbs, if desired, and serve.

ⓥ Per serving (prepared as pictured, opposite): 318 calories, 15.69 g fat (1.94 g saturated fat), 0 mg cholesterol, 35.21 g carbohydrates, 14.34 g protein, 5.9 g fiber

Spring Vegetable Ragout

The next time you find yourself with a bounty of produce from your Community Supported Agriculture (CSA) group or farmer's market, try this ultra-quick ragout; it takes fewer than ten minutes from start to finish. This recipe calls for spring vegetables; for a summer variation, try string beans, corn, and zucchini. Serve the ragout over pasta, polenta, or brown rice, and if you like, sprinkle with finely grated cheese. **SERVES 4**

1 tablespoon olive oil

3 leeks, white and pale-green parts only, halved lengthwise, thinly sliced into half-moons (about 2 cups), washed well and drained

Coarse salt

12 ounces asparagus, tough ends trimmed, cut into 1-inch pieces (about 2½ cups)

1 cup water

6 ounces sugar snap peas, trimmed and cut into 1-inch pieces (about 1½ cups)

8 radishes, quartered

1 teaspoon Dijon mustard

1 tablespoon unsalted butter

1 tablespoon minced fresh herbs, such as chives and tarragon

1. Heat olive oil in a large skillet over medium-high. Add leeks and season with salt; sauté until leeks are tender, stirring frequently, about 2 minutes. Stir in asparagus, then the water. Simmer, covered, 2 minutes. Add snap peas and radishes; cover, and simmer until vegetables are just tender, about 2 minutes more.

2. Stir in mustard until well combined, then swirl in butter and herbs. Serve immediately.

Ⓖ Per serving: 140 calories, 6.5 g fat (2.3 g saturated fat), 7.5 mg cholesterol, 16.84 g carbohydrates, 4 g protein, 4.1 g fiber

Potato and Zucchini Hash

Your favorite breakfast foods can work equally well for dinner. Here, sliced zucchini perks up potato hash topped with a fried egg, cooked sunny side up (or poached; see page 363). **SERVES 4**

2 russet potatoes (1½ pounds total), peeled, quartered lengthwise, and thinly sliced crosswise

2 tablespoons olive oil

½ yellow onion, thinly sliced

Coarse salt and freshly ground pepper

1 zucchini, quartered lengthwise and thinly sliced crosswise

1 tablespoon unsalted butter

4 large eggs

1. Rinse potato slices well under cold running water, then drain and thoroughly pat dry. In a large nonstick skillet, heat olive oil over medium-high. Add onion and potatoes and season with salt and pepper. Cook, stirring frequently, until potatoes are almost cooked through and golden, about 15 minutes.

2. Add zucchini, reduce heat to medium, and cook, stirring, until zucchini is soft and potatoes are cooked through, about 7 minutes. Season with salt and pepper.

3. Meanwhile, heat a large skillet over medium. Add butter. Once butter begins to sizzle, crack eggs into pan and cook until whites are just set and golden brown at the edges, about 3 minutes. Divide hash among 4 plates, top each with an egg, and serve.

Ⓖ Per serving: 312 calories, 15.1 g fat (4.4 g saturated fat), 219 mg cholesterol, 35.05 g carbohydrates, 11.08 g protein, 3.32 g fiber

Brown-Rice Stir-Fry with Marinated Tofu

Stir-fries are fast, make good use of fresh vegetables, and get their flavor from basic items like soy sauce, ginger, and garlic. This egg-free version is made with colorful bell peppers, but practically any vegetable will work, including broccoli, string beans, carrots, snap peas, and bok choy. **SERVES 4**

2 tablespoons canola or safflower oil

3 garlic cloves, minced

1 piece (about 3 inches) fresh ginger, peeled and finely chopped

½ recipe Marinated Tofu (page 365), cut into 1-inch cubes

2 bell peppers (1 red and 1 yellow), ribs and seeds removed, cut into 1-inch chunks

3 cups cooked brown rice (see page 371)

3 tablespoons low-sodium soy sauce

1 tablespoon toasted-sesame oil

Coarse salt and freshly ground pepper

3 scallions, trimmed, halved lengthwise, and thinly sliced

1 In a wok or large skillet, heat the canola oil over medium-high. Add garlic and ginger; cook, stirring, until fragrant, about 30 seconds.

2 Add tofu, and cook, stirring, until golden brown, about 2 minutes. Add bell peppers; cook, stirring, until peppers are crisp-tender, about 3 minutes.

3 Add rice and soy sauce; cook, stirring frequently, until rice is heated through, about 3 minutes. Stir in sesame oil. Season with salt and pepper; garnish with scallions and serve.

V Per serving: 430 calories, 23.54 g fat (2.91 g saturated fat), 0 mg cholesterol, 43.4 g carbohydrates, 14.48 g protein, 4.44 g fiber

Scrambled Tofu with Collards

Thanks to a pinch of turmeric, tofu takes on the same color as eggs in a quick scramble that also features collard greens sautéed with fresh ginger and garlic. Try it served over brown rice, on a slice of rustic bread, or wrapped in a tortilla. You can also substitute other greens, such as kale or Swiss chard, for the collards. **SERVES 2**

1 tablespoon extra-virgin olive oil

2 garlic cloves, minced

½ red onion, chopped

½ teaspoon ground turmeric

1 teaspoon grated peeled fresh ginger

3 collard green leaves, stems removed, cut into ½-inch pieces

2 tablespoons water

7 ounces (½ package) firm tofu, drained and crumbled

Coarse salt and freshly ground pepper

1 Heat olive oil in a large skillet over medium. Cook garlic, onion, turmeric, and ginger until onion is tender, stirring frequently, 3 to 4 minutes. Stir in collard greens and the water and cook, stirring, until greens are bright green and tender, about 2 minutes.

2 Add crumbled tofu and cook, stirring, until heated through, about 2 minutes. Season with salt and pepper and serve.

V G Per serving: 174 calories, 12.93 g fat (1.56 g saturated fat), 0 mg cholesterol, 6.59 g carbohydrates, 10.59 g protein, 1.39 g fiber

Broccoli-and-Cheese Over-Easy Omelet

To make this "over-easy" omelet, a whole egg and two whites are cooked atop a layer of melted cheese, without first being whisked together, until the whites are just set. The yolk is left runny so it acts as a rich "sauce." Because it is thin (almost like a crepe), the omelet can easily be folded over the filling. You can use other vegetables in place of broccoli—zucchini, cauliflower, mushrooms, and spinach are all good options; just sauté them first. **MAKES 1**

½ teaspoon olive oil

1¼ cups thinly sliced broccoli florets

1 scallion, trimmed and thinly sliced on the bias

Coarse salt and freshly ground pepper

1 tablespoon plus 1 teaspoon finely grated Parmigiano-Reggiano

1 large whole egg plus 2 large egg whites

Pinch of crushed red pepper flakes

1 Heat olive oil in a medium skillet over medium. Add broccoli and scallion and cover pan; cook, stirring occasionally, until tender, about 4 minutes. Season with salt and pepper. Transfer to a plate.

2 Add cheese to skillet. Cook over medium-high until melted and golden, about 1 minute. Reduce heat to medium-low. Add whole egg and whites. Keeping egg yolk intact, drag a spatula through the whites to spread them evenly in the pan. Cook, covered, until whites are set and yolk is still runny, 1 to 1½ minutes.

3 Top eggs with broccoli-scallion mixture, and fold omelet over. Slide onto a plate, sprinkle with a pinch of red pepper flakes, and serve.

G Per serving: 192 calories, 9 g fat (3 g saturated fat), 217 mg cholesterol, 9 g carbohydrates, 22 g protein, 3 g fiber

Brown Rice with Black Beans and Avocado

Rice and beans, a beautifully balanced source of complete protein, get extra substance when made with brown rice and black beans (which have more fiber than any other legume). **SERVES 6**

FOR THE BEANS

- 1 pound dried black beans, soaked and drained (see page 365)
- 1 jalapeño chile, halved and seeded
- 2 onions, quartered
- 5 garlic cloves, smashed
- 2 tablespoons red-wine vinegar
  Coarse salt and freshly ground pepper

FOR THE RICE

- ¼ cup olive oil
- 1 onion, finely chopped
- 1 garlic clove, minced
  Coarse salt and freshly ground pepper
- 2 cups long-grain brown rice

FOR SERVING

Assorted garnishes, such as fresh cilantro, diced red onion, chopped tomato, cubed avocado, sour cream, and hot sauce

1 Make the beans: Bring 8 cups water, beans, jalapeño, onions, garlic, vinegar, 1 tablespoon salt, and 1 teaspoon pepper to a simmer in a medium pot. Cook, stirring occasionally, until beans are tender, about 1½ hours. (Add more water, ¼ cup at a time, if needed to cover beans.) Season with salt and pepper.

2 Meanwhile, make the rice: Heat olive oil in a medium saucepan over medium-high. Cook onion and garlic until onion is soft, stirring frequently, about 5 minutes. Add 2 teaspoons salt, ¼ teaspoon pepper, and the rice. Cook until rice is lightly toasted, about 3 minutes. Add 3½ cups water, and bring to a boil. Reduce heat to low, and gently simmer, covered, until rice is tender and absorbs water, 25 to 30 minutes. Remove from heat; let stand, covered, 10 minutes. Fluff rice with a fork.

3 To serve, divide rice and beans evenly among 6 bowls and top with assorted garnishes, as desired.

Ⓖ Per serving: 566 calories, 11.82 g fat (1.87 g saturated fat), 0 mg cholesterol, 94.73 g carbohydrates, 21.5 g protein, 18.47 g fiber

Frittata with Asparagus, Goat Cheese, and Herbs

A frittata is a boon to the home cook: it's flexible enough to go from midweek family supper to weekend brunch with friends, and it suits pretty much any other occasion that calls for something delicious and unfussy. And frittatas need not be served right away, given that they taste equally good warm or at room temperature. **SERVES 6**

½ bunch asparagus (about 8 ounces), tough ends trimmed, tips cut into 2- to 3-inch pieces, stalks cut into ½-inch pieces

Coarse salt and freshly ground pepper

12 large eggs

4 scallions, trimmed and thinly sliced

2 tablespoons snipped fresh chives

2 tablespoons olive oil

2 ounces fresh goat cheese (about ¼ cup)

1 Prepare an ice-water bath. Blanch asparagus in a pot of boiling salted water until just tender, about 1 minute. Drain and transfer to the ice bath to stop the cooking. Drain.

2 Preheat oven to 425°F. Whisk eggs with 1 teaspoon each salt and pepper in a medium bowl. Stir in scallions, chives, and asparagus stalks.

3 Heat olive oil in an ovenproof 10-inch skillet (preferably cast-iron) over medium. Pour egg mixture into skillet. Cook until edges begin to set, then push cooked eggs around the edge toward the center of the pan with a wooden spoon. Continue cooking until the center begins to set, about 2 minutes more.

4 Dollop goat cheese over top and sprinkle with asparagus tips. Bake until eggs are completely set, 8 to 10 minutes. Let cool slightly before serving.

G Per serving: 216 calories, 16 g fat (5 g saturated fat), 376 mg cholesterol, 2 g carbohydrates, 15 g protein, 1 g fiber

Southwestern Hash

Despite its origins as a meat-centric dish, hash is just as satisfying as the center of a vegetarian meal—especially when nutty, chewy tempeh is included. Black beans supply additional protein to this recipe, made with jalapeño, cumin, and other Southwestern staples. **SERVES 4**

2 red potatoes (12 ounces), scrubbed and cut into 1-inch pieces

Coarse salt and freshly ground pepper

3 tablespoons canola oil

½ teaspoon ground cumin

1 jalapeño chile, finely diced (ribs and seeds removed for less heat if desired)

3 scallions, trimmed and thinly sliced

8 ounces cherry tomatoes, halved

1½ cups cooked black beans (see page 365), drained and rinsed

2 teaspoons nutritional yeast seasoning (see note, page 168)

1 package (8 ounces) plain, pasteurized organic tempeh

1 firm, ripe avocado, halved, pitted, peeled, and coarsely chopped

1 Bring potatoes to a boil in a pot of salted water. Cook until knife-tender, about 6 minutes; drain.

2 Heat 2 tablespoons oil in a large saucepan over medium-high. Add cumin and cook, stirring, until fragrant, about 30 seconds. Add potatoes and cook, stirring occasionally, until golden, 5 to 7 minutes. Transfer to a bowl.

3 Heat remaining tablespoon oil over medium. Add jalapeño, scallions (reserve 1 for garnish if desired), tomatoes, beans, and yeast; crumble in tempeh. Cook until tomatoes begin to break down, stirring frequently, 5 to 7 minutes. Add potatoes and cook just until heated through. Remove pan from heat and gently stir in avocado. Season with salt and pepper. Garnish with reserved scallion, if desired, and serve.

V G Per serving: 457 calories, 24 g fat (3 g saturated fat), 0 mg cholesterol, 46 g carbohydrates, 19 g protein, 11 g fiber

Shiitake Fried Rice

Fried rice is a restaurant standby that's easy to make at home, especially if you have leftover rice. It's also open to many interpretations, depending on the vegetables in your crisper (think carrots, broccoli, and snap peas). Frozen edamame is a handy shortcut; keep some in the freezer for adding protein to other stir-fries, as well as to soups and salads. **SERVES 4**

1 tablespoon plus 1 teaspoon canola oil

2 large eggs, lightly beaten

Coarse salt and freshly ground pepper

1 pound shiitake mushrooms, stemmed, thinly sliced

3 garlic cloves, minced

2 tablespoons minced peeled fresh ginger

¼ to ½ teaspoon crushed red pepper flakes

4 cups cooked brown rice (see page 371)

1 cup frozen shelled edamame, thawed

4 scallions, trimmed and thinly sliced

3 tablespoons fresh lime juice (from 2 to 3 limes)

2 tablespoons low-sodium soy sauce

1. In a large nonstick skillet, heat 1 teaspoon oil over medium. Add eggs; season with salt and pepper. Cook until set, 1 to 3 minutes. Transfer to a cutting board and let cool; roll up and thinly slice crosswise.

2. In same skillet, heat remaining tablespoon oil over medium-high. Add mushrooms, garlic, ginger, and red pepper flakes; season with salt. Cook, tossing frequently, until mushrooms are tender, 2 to 4 minutes. Add rice, eggs, edamame, scallions, lime juice, and soy sauce. Cook, tossing, until rice is heated through, 2 to 3 minutes. Serve immediately.

Per serving: 456 calories, 11 g fat (1.5 g saturated fat), 105.75 mg cholesterol, 71 g carbohydrates, 16 g protein, 8 g fiber

Black Bean and Millet Bowl with Vegetables

Here's another interpretation of a so-called "bowl" (see Buddha Bowl, page 69) that combines all the components of a healthy plant-based diet in one very wholesome dish. **SERVES 2**

FOR THE MILLET

- ¼ cup millet
- 1½ cups cooked black beans (see page 365), drained and rinsed
- 2 tablespoons minced peeled fresh ginger

  Coarse salt and freshly ground pepper

FOR THE VEGETABLES

- 4 shiitake mushrooms, stemmed and thinly sliced
- 1 carrot, peeled and thinly sliced
- 2 heads baby bok choy, halved
- ½ cup shredded red cabbage
- 1 scallion, trimmed and thinly sliced

FOR THE DRESSING

- 3 tablespoons extra-virgin olive oil
- 3 tablespoons apple cider vinegar

  Coarse salt

- 2 tablespoons toasted sunflower seeds (see page 363)

1 Make the millet: Place millet, black beans, and ginger in a small saucepan. Add ½ teaspoon salt and 1 cup water. Bring to a boil, stir once, then reduce heat and simmer, covered, 25 minutes. Let rest 10 minutes, then fluff with a fork.

2 Make the vegetables: Place shiitakes in a steamer basket or colander set over 2 inches boiling water in a medium pot; cover and steam 3 minutes. Add carrots and bok choy and steam, covered, 4 to 6 minutes more. Remove from heat.

3 Make the dressing: In a small bowl, whisk together olive oil and vinegar. Season with a pinch of salt.

4 To serve, divide millet mixture among 2 bowls. Top with cabbage, scallion, and steamed vegetables; season with salt and pepper. Drizzle with dressing and sprinkle with sunflower seeds.

V G S Per serving: 672 calories, 26 g fat (4 g saturated fat), 89 g carbohydrates, 0 mg cholesterol, 23.83 g protein, 20.36 g fiber

Vegetable-Egg Donburi

Donburi is a popular Japanese dish of rice topped with meat, fish, or eggs, as in this vegetable-rich version. Here, whole eggs (and additional whites) are cooked along with mushrooms, snow peas, carrot, and scallions in the manner of an easy, no-stir omelet. It's worth seeking out radish sprouts for their peppery flavor, but other types of sprouts will also work. **SERVES 4**

2 large whole eggs plus 4 large egg whites

Pinch of freshly ground pepper

1 teaspoon canola oil

6 shiitake mushrooms, stemmed and thinly sliced

10 snow peas

1 carrot, peeled and julienned with vegetable peeler

3 scallions, white parts thinly sliced, green parts cut into 1½-inch lengths

1½ cups vegetable stock, preferably homemade (see page 364)

1½ teaspoons grated peeled fresh ginger

2 tablespoons low-sodium soy sauce

2 cups cooked brown rice (see page 371)

1 ounce radish sprouts

1 Lightly whisk together whole eggs, whites, and pepper in a medium bowl. Heat oil in a medium nonstick skillet over medium-high. Sauté mushrooms until browned, stirring frequently, 2 to 3 minutes. Add the snow peas, carrot, and scallions. Cook, stirring, until snow peas turn bright green, about 1 minute.

2 Add the vegetable stock, ginger, and soy sauce to skillet. Cook until liquid has been reduced by half, about 6 minutes. Gently pour in the reserved egg mixture without stirring. Cover skillet, and cook until eggs have just set, 4 to 5 minutes. Remove from heat.

3 To serve, divide the rice among 4 soup bowls. Divide omelet into 4 servings; spoon omelet and any remaining broth over the rice. Garnish with radish sprouts and serve.

Per serving: 385 calories, 3 g fat (1 g saturated fat), 107 mg cholesterol, 76 g carbohydrates, 15 g protein, 2 g fiber

Black-Rice Stir-Fry

Black rice transforms a take-out favorite into a dish worthy of a dinner party. Black rice is available at Asian food markets and many supermarkets; brown rice can be substituted. **SERVES 4**

1 cup black rice, rinsed
Coarse salt

3 tablespoons canola oil

14 ounces (1 package) firm tofu, drained and pressed (see page 363), cut into ½-inch pieces

1 Japanese eggplant, halved lengthwise and cut into ½-inch pieces

2 tablespoons minced peeled fresh ginger

2 garlic cloves, minced

3 scallions, thinly sliced

¼ head red cabbage, sliced (4 cups)

½ bunch purple kale, torn into 2-inch pieces

1 teaspoon Asian hot chile sauce, preferably Sriracha

1 tablespoon low-sodium soy sauce

2 tablespoons fresh lime juice (from 1 to 2 limes)

1 Bring rice, 1¾ cups water, and ½ teaspoon salt to a boil in a large saucepan. Reduce heat to low and cook until rice is tender and has absorbed all water, about 35 minutes. Remove from heat, cover, and let stand 10 minutes. Fluff with a fork.

2 Heat a wok or large skillet over medium-high 1 minute. Add 1 tablespoon oil, swirling. Season tofu with salt and cook, tossing, until golden and crisp, about 5 minutes. Transfer to a plate. Add 1 tablespoon oil and cook eggplant, stirring, until golden, about 4 minutes. Transfer to plate.

3 Add remaining tablespoon oil and cook ginger, garlic, and scallions 1 minute. Add cabbage, kale, and ¼ cup water and cook until kale is tender, about 3 minutes.

4 Mix in rice and cook, stirring, until heated through. Add tofu and eggplant. Stir in chile sauce and soy sauce. Remove from heat; stir in lime juice, and serve.

V Per serving: 235 calories, 11.5 g fat (1.5 g saturated fat), 0 mg cholesterol, 24 g carbohydrates, 11 g protein, 3 g fiber

Harvest Vegetable Galette with Greens and Goat Cheese

Bring vibrant color and sweetness to an ordinary potato pancake with grated beets and carrots. This protein-rich version also includes chickpeas, and is lovely as the foundation for a mixed green salad. **SERVES 4**

1 russet potato, scrubbed and diced

3 large beets (1½ pounds), scrubbed and peeled

3 carrots

1½ cups cooked chickpeas (see page 365), drained and rinsed, half coarsely chopped

½ cup all-purpose flour

Coarse salt and freshly ground pepper

3 tablespoons olive oil

5 ounces mixed salad greens

1 tablespoon fresh lemon juice

2 ounces fresh goat cheese, crumbled (¼ cup)

1 Bring potato to a boil in a pot of salted water. Cook until knife-tender, about 6 minutes; drain.

2 Grate beets and carrots on the large holes of a box grater into a large bowl (or shred in a food processor). Stir in chickpeas, potato, flour, and 1 teaspoon salt. Season with pepper.

3 In a large nonstick straight-sided skillet, heat 1 tablespoon olive oil over medium. Add beet mixture and, with a flexible spatula, firmly press evenly into pan. Cook, undisturbed, 10 minutes. Remove pan from heat, cover with a serving platter, and carefully invert pancake onto platter. Slide pancake back into pan and cook until crisp and brown around edge, 10 to 12 minutes. Invert pancake onto platter.

4 In a medium bowl, toss salad greens with remaining 2 tablespoons oil and the lemon juice. Season with salt and pepper. Top pancake with salad and goat cheese and cut into wedges to serve.

Per serving: 419 calories, 15 g fat (4 g saturated fat), 6.52 mg cholesterol, 60 g carbohydrates, 13 g protein, 10 g fiber

Spiced Tofu with Wilted Spinach and Yogurt

Saag paneer, an Indian vegetarian dish, is the inspiration for this lighter, more convenient version made with tofu in the place of the traditional soft, ripened cheese. **SERVES 4**

2 tablespoons canola oil

12 ounces (¾ package) firm tofu, drained, pressed (see page 363), and cut into 1-inch cubes

Coarse salt

1 onion, diced

3 garlic cloves, minced

1 teaspoon grated peeled fresh ginger

½ teaspoon cumin seeds, crushed

½ teaspoon coriander seeds, crushed

¼ teaspoon mustard seeds, crushed

Pinch of crushed red pepper flakes

1½ pounds fresh spinach, stemmed and chopped

1 cup plain low-fat yogurt

2 cups cooked brown rice (see page 371)

1 In a large cast-iron skillet, heat 1 tablespoon oil over medium-high. Add tofu and cook, turning, until golden brown, about 7 minutes. Transfer to a plate and season with salt.

2 Heat remaining tablespoon oil in a large pot over medium-high. Add onion and garlic and cook, stirring, until tender, about 5 minutes. Add ginger and spices and cook, stirring, until spices are toasted, about 1 minute. Add spinach and cook, stirring, until just wilted, 2 to 3 minutes.

3 Remove from heat and stir in yogurt. Season with salt and stir in golden tofu. Serve with rice.

G Per serving: 450 calories, 15 g fat (2 g saturated fat), 5 mg cholesterol, 65 g carbohydrates, 21 g protein, 12 g fiber

Polenta with Poached Eggs and Marinated Artichokes

Polenta, a staple of Italy, is often overlooked as a whole-grain option for savory meals, but it is a versatile accompaniment to many vegetables and pairs particularly well with eggs. **SERVES 4**

6 artichoke hearts (fresh, jarred, or frozen and thawed), quartered

3 tablespoons extra-virgin olive oil

1 tablespoon red-wine vinegar

2 tablespoons chopped fresh flat-leaf parsley leaves

Crushed red pepper flakes

Coarse salt and freshly ground black pepper

1 cup milk

3 cups water, plus more if needed

¾ cup medium-grain polenta

2 tablespoons freshly grated Parmigiano-Reggiano

4 large eggs

1 Combine artichokes with 2 tablespoons olive oil, the vinegar, parsley, and red pepper flakes. Season with salt and let marinate at room temperature.

2 Bring milk and the water to a boil in a large saucepan. Gradually add polenta and cook, stirring constantly, until liquid is absorbed and polenta is tender, 18 to 20 minutes. Remove from heat and stir in remaining oil and cheese. Season with salt and pepper and cover. (If polenta becomes too thick, whisk in more water, 1 tablespoon at a time.)

3 Fill a high-sided skillet with 2 inches water; bring to a boil, then reduce to a simmer. Crack 1 egg at a time into a teacup and gently slide into simmering water. Repeat with remaining eggs. Cook until whites are just set and yolks are still loose, 3 to 4 minutes. Remove eggs from water using a slotted spoon.

4 Divide polenta among 4 serving bowls. Top each bowl with an egg and artichokes. Serve immediately.

Ⓖ Per serving: 336 calories, 17 g fat (4 g saturated fat), 217 mg cholesterol, 33 g carbohydrates, 13 g protein, 4 g fiber

VERSATILE VEGETARIAN:
RISOTTO

Making risotto is a simple process to master—albeit with lots of careful stirring. Risotto is ready when it has a loose consistency; it should ripple when spooned onto a plate. Traditional versions use Arborio or Carnaroli rice; farro and pearl barley are other good options (see page 102).

TOAST RICE · ADD STOCK · FINISH DISH

ASPARAGUS AND LEMON RISOTTO SERVES 4

6 cups vegetable stock, preferably homemade (see page 364)

¼ cup olive oil

1 small onion, finely chopped

1 cup Arborio rice

½ cup dry white wine

1 bunch asparagus, trimmed, stalks cut into 1-inch lengths

1 cup thawed frozen peas

1 teaspoon grated lemon zest, plus more for garnish

2 tablespoons fresh lemon juice

1 cup chopped fresh flat-leaf parsley leaves

½ cup finely grated Parmigiano-Reggiano, plus more for serving

Coarse salt and freshly ground pepper

1. Bring stock to a simmer in a medium saucepan.

2. Heat 2 tablespoons olive oil over medium in another saucepan. Cook onion, stirring frequently, until soft, 6 to 7 minutes. Add rice, cook, stirring, until edges are translucent, 2 to 3 minutes. Add wine; cook, stirring, just until evaporated.

3. Add ½ cup hot stock; cook, stirring, until almost absorbed. Continue adding ½ cup stock in this manner until liquid is creamy and rice is al dente, about 20 minutes total (you may not need to add all of the stock). Add asparagus with the last addition of stock, and the peas about 1 minute before risotto is done.

4. Remove from heat; stir in lemon zest and juice, parsley, cheese, and remaining 2 tablespoons oil. Season with salt and pepper. Serve immediately with additional cheese and lemon zest.

G Per serving: 467 calories, 17.62 g fat (3.76 g saturated fat), 8.8 mg cholesterol, 59.4 g carbohydrates, 13.64 g protein, 7.86 g fiber

Farro Risotto with Wild Mushrooms SERVES 4

3½ cups vegetable stock, preferably homemade (see page 364)

4 cups water

¼ cup extra-virgin olive oil

8 ounces mixed mushrooms such as shiitake, cremini, and hen of the woods, stemmed and halved if large

1 tablespoon fresh thyme leaves

Coarse salt and freshly ground pepper

½ small onion, finely chopped

1 cup farro

⅓ cup dry white wine

½ cup finely grated Parmigiano-Reggiano

1. Bring stock and the water to a simmer in a medium saucepan.

2. Heat 1 tablespoon olive oil in a large skillet over medium-high. Add half the mushrooms and thyme; cook, stirring, until mushrooms are golden and tender, about 5 minutes. Season with salt and pepper. Transfer to a plate. Repeat with another tablespoon oil and remaining mushrooms and thyme. Keep warm.

3. Heat remaining 2 tablespoons oil in a medium pot over medium. Cook onion, stirring, until softened, 3 to 4 minutes. Add farro and cook, stirring, 1 to 2 minutes. Add wine and cook, stirring, just until evaporated.

4. Add ½ cup hot stock mixture to the pot. Cook, stirring, until almost absorbed. Continue adding stock in this manner until farro is tender but firm to the bite and mixture is creamy, 20 to 30 minutes. Stir in cheese and season with salt. Divide evenly among 4 bowls, top with mushroom mixture, and serve.

Per serving: 389 calories, 16.44 g fat (3.61 g saturated fat), 8.8 mg cholesterol, 44.1 g carbohydrates, 13.3 g protein, 4.45 g fiber

Pearl Barley Risotto with Corn and Basil SERVES 4

3½ cups vegetable stock, preferably homemade (see page 364)

4 cups water

2 tablespoons olive oil

1 onion, finely chopped

Coarse salt and freshly ground pepper

1 cup pearl barley

½ cup dry white wine

1½ cups fresh corn kernels or 1 package (10 ounces) frozen corn, thawed

½ cup grated Parmigiano-Reggiano, plus more for serving

1 cup packed fresh basil leaves

1. Bring stock and the water to a simmer in a medium saucepan.

2. Meanwhile, heat olive oil in a large saucepan over medium. Add onion and season with salt and pepper; cook, stirring occasionally, until onion is softened, 4 to 5 minutes. Add barley and cook, stirring, until toasted, about 1 minute. Add wine; cook, stirring, just until evaporated, about 1 minute.

3. Using a ladle, add 2 cups hot stock mixture; simmer, stirring occasionally, until almost absorbed, 10 to 12 minutes. Continue adding stock mixture, ½ cup at a time, until barley is tender and mixture is creamy, 40 to 50 minutes (you may not have to use all the stock). Add corn; cook just to heat through, stirring occasionally, 4 to 5 minutes.

4. Stir in cheese; season with salt and pepper. Serve immediately, garnished with basil and additional cheese.

Ⓖ Per serving: 426 calories, 11.98 g fat (3.6 g saturated fat), 12.47 mg cholesterol, 64.51 g carbohydrates, 13.83 g protein, 10.98 g fiber

soups, stews, and chili

White Bean and Mushroom Stew

Rosemary and white beans are a winning combination. Here they are simmered with tomatoes and mushrooms to make a rustic stew for cool-weather meals. **SERVES 4**

2 tablespoons olive oil, plus more for drizzling

1 onion, coarsely chopped

1 celery stalk, diced

1 carrot, peeled and diced

1 pound cremini mushrooms, quartered

½ cup dry white wine

1 can (28 ounces) whole peeled tomatoes, pureed in a blender

1 sprig rosemary

2 cups cooked white beans (see page 365), drained and rinsed

½ cup water

Coarse salt and freshly ground pepper

1 Heat olive oil in a medium saucepan over medium. Cook onion, celery, and carrot until tender, stirring occasionally, about 8 minutes.

2 Raise heat to medium-high, add mushrooms, and cook, stirring often, until softened, 5 to 7 minutes. Add wine to pan, scraping up any brown bits with a wooden spoon.

3 Add tomatoes, rosemary, beans, and the water. Bring to a boil; reduce heat and simmer until slightly thickened, about 15 minutes. Discard rosemary sprig. Season with salt and pepper. Serve hot, drizzled with olive oil.

V G S Per serving: 195 calories, 5 g fat (1 g saturated fat), 0 mg cholesterol, 26 g carbohydrates, 9 g protein, 6 g fiber

Thirty-Clove Garlic Soup

Garlic is a well-known immunity-boosting powerhouse and may help ward off colds. Make a big batch of this velvety soup and keep it in the freezer for whenever you need a restorative kick. Serve with toasted rustic bread. **SERVES 4**

- 2 heads garlic, halved crosswise
- 1 tablespoon extra-virgin olive oil
- 4 cups vegetable stock, preferably homemade (see page 364)
- 8 ounces Yukon gold potatoes, peeled and chopped
- ¼ cup freshly grated Parmigiano-Reggiano, plus more for serving

    Coarse salt and freshly ground pepper

1. Preheat oven to 375°F. Drizzle garlic heads with olive oil. Wrap tightly in parchment, then foil, and roast until tender, about 40 minutes. Let cool, then squeeze cloves from papery skins.

2. Bring stock, potatoes, and roasted garlic to a boil in a medium saucepan; reduce heat and simmer until potatoes are tender, about 12 minutes. Remove from heat and stir in cheese.

3. Let cool slightly. Working in batches, puree in a blender until smooth, being careful not to fill jar more than halfway each time. Season with salt and pepper. Reheat before serving with additional cheese.

Per serving: 150 calories, 6 g fat (2 g saturated fat), 9 mg cholesterol, 19 g carbohydrates, 9 g protein, 2 g fiber

Chilled Avocado Soup

Avocado's smooth texture makes it a natural candidate for blending into creamy, full-bodied soups, like this one, which is tangy with buttermilk. No pots, pans, or even mixing bowls are required; just toss the raw ingredients into the blender and press "puree." **SERVES 4**

3 firm, ripe avocados

2 cups low-fat buttermilk

⅓ cup walnuts

⅓ cup dill sprigs, plus more for garnish (optional)

⅓ cup diced red onion (about ½ small onion)

1 tablespoon red-wine vinegar

Coarse salt

1 cup water

1 Halve and pit 2 avocados. With a spoon, scoop out flesh and transfer to a blender. Add buttermilk, walnuts, dill, red onion, vinegar, 1 teaspoon salt, and the water and puree until smooth. Cover the blender and refrigerate until the soup is well chilled, at least 1 hour and up to overnight.

2 To serve, halve and pit remaining avocado. Quarter lengthwise, and then cut crosswise into ½-inch pieces. Season soup with salt and divide among 4 bowls. Garnish each with diced avocado and, if desired, more dill.

Ⓖ Per serving: 352 calories, 29 g fat (4.39 g saturated fat), 4.9 mg cholesterol, 22 g carbohydrates, 8 g protein, 11 g fiber

Smooth Tomato Gazpacho

The Spanish antidote to summer's heat, gazpacho owes its characteristic freshness to peak-of-season tomatoes and cucumbers, flavored with garlic, onion, and a splash of sherry vinegar. Almonds add body and rich flavor to this version. **SERVES 4**

2 pounds tomatoes (about 4), cored and chopped

½ English cucumber, peeled and chopped

½ onion, chopped

1 small garlic clove

2 ounces blanched almonds (about ½ cup), toasted (see page 363)

¼ cup water

2 tablespoons sherry vinegar

2 tablespoons extra-virgin olive oil, plus more for drizzling

Coarse salt and freshly ground pepper

1 Puree tomatoes, cucumber, onion, garlic, almonds, the water, vinegar, olive oil, and 2¼ teaspoons salt in a blender until smooth; season with pepper.

2 Refrigerate in an airtight container at least 45 minutes or up to 2 days. Drizzle with oil and season with salt and pepper just before serving.

V G Per serving: 259 calories, 21.68 g fat (2.59 g saturated fat), 0 mg cholesterol, 14.15 g carbohydrates, 5.49 g protein, 4.55 g fiber

Roasted Red Pepper Soup with Quinoa Salsa

An unconventional quinoa, avocado, and cilantro salsa lends complementary flavors and textures—as well as protein—to this warm soup. **SERVES 4**

2 tablespoons olive oil

1 yellow onion, chopped

2 garlic cloves, sliced

Pinch of crushed red pepper flakes

4 red bell peppers, roasted and quartered (see page 364)

3 cups vegetable stock, preferably homemade (see page 364)

Coarse salt

1 cup cooked quinoa (see page 371)

¼ small red onion, diced

1 firm, ripe avocado, halved, pitted, peeled, and diced

2 tablespoons chopped fresh cilantro leaves

Lime wedges, for serving

1. Heat olive oil in a medium saucepan over medium. Add yellow onion, garlic, and red pepper flakes and cook, stirring occasionally, until onion is tender, 6 to 8 minutes. Add roasted peppers and stock. Bring to a boil; reduce heat and simmer 10 minutes.

2. Let cool slightly. Working in batches, puree soup in a blender until smooth, being careful not to fill jar more than halfway each time. Reheat after blending, and season with salt.

3. In a small bowl, mix together quinoa, red onion, avocado, and cilantro. Season with salt. To serve, divide soup among 4 bowls, top with quinoa salsa, and squeeze with lime.

V G S Per serving: 165 calories, 10 g fat (2 g saturated fat), 3 mg cholesterol, 17 g carbohydrates, 5 g protein, 5 g fiber

Stewed Lentils with Yogurt and Cucumbers

It takes less than half an hour to make this pared-down version of Indian daal topped with yogurt and diced cucumber. **SERVES 4**

FOR THE LENTILS

- 1 teaspoon cumin seeds
- 2 tablespoons olive oil
- 1 cup diced onion
- 4 garlic cloves, minced
- 2 tablespoons minced peeled fresh ginger
- 1 teaspoon turmeric
- 2 cups dried red lentils, picked over and rinsed

  Coarse salt

FOR SERVING

- ¼ cup diced onion
- 1 cup diced cucumber (peeled and seeded)
- 1 fresh green chile, thinly sliced (ribs and seeds removed for less heat, if desired)
- ¼ cup chopped fresh cilantro, plus leaves for garnish
- 1 tablespoon white vinegar

  Coarse salt

- 4 cups cooked brown basmati rice (see page 371)
- 1 cup plain Greek-style yogurt (2 percent)

1 Make the lentils: Heat a medium saucepan over medium. Add cumin seeds and toast, swirling pan, until fragrant, about 1 minute; transfer to a plate. Add olive oil; once hot, add onion, garlic, and ginger. Cook, stirring often, until tender, about 5 minutes. Add turmeric and toasted seeds. Cook, stirring, 1 minute.

2 Add 5 cups water and the lentils. Bring to a boil; reduce to a simmer and partially cover. Cook until lentils are tender and mixture thickens, about 15 minutes. Season with salt.

3 Meanwhile, combine onion, cucumber, chile, chopped cilantro, and vinegar in a bowl; season with salt.

4 To serve, divide rice among 4 bowls and ladle lentils over rice; top with yogurt and the cucumber mixture. Garnish with cilantro leaves.

G Per serving: 652 calories, 10 g fat (2 g saturated fat), 3 mg cholesterol, 109 g carbohydrates, 36 g protein, 18.7 g fiber

Lentil and Sweet-Potato Stew

Lentils are a good choice for making vegetarian stews, since they don't require presoaking and take much less time to cook than other legumes. Here they are combined with sweet potatoes and other vegetables in a dish with Indian flavors. **SERVES 6**

2 tablespoons canola oil

1 onion, chopped

2 carrots, peeled and chopped

2 celery stalks, chopped

1 bay leaf

1 garlic clove, minced

1½ teaspoons curry powder

2 cups dried brown lentils, picked over and rinsed

2 sweet potatoes (about 1 pound), peeled and cut into ½-inch dice

9 ounces fresh green beans, cut into ½-inch pieces

1 can (14½ ounces) diced tomatoes in juice

½ cup chopped fresh cilantro, plus leaves for garnish

Coarse salt and freshly ground pepper

Plain low-fat yogurt, for serving

1 In a large saucepan, heat oil over medium-high. Add onion, carrots, celery, and bay leaf. Cook, stirring often, until vegetables are softened, 5 to 7 minutes. Add garlic and curry powder and cook, stirring, until fragrant, about 1 minute more.

2 Add 7 cups water and the lentils and bring to a boil. Reduce to a simmer, cover, and cook 10 minutes. Add potatoes and continue to cook, covered, until lentils and potatoes are just tender, about 15 minutes.

3 Stir in green beans and tomatoes with their juice. Cook until warmed through, 2 to 4 minutes. Discard bay leaf. Add chopped cilantro; season with salt and pepper. Serve topped with yogurt and garnished with cilantro leaves.

G Per serving: 345 calories, 6 g fat (0.4 g saturated fat), 0 mg cholesterol, 57 g carbohydrates, 19 g protein, 18 g fiber

Green Vegetable Curry

Store-bought curry pastes, sold in cans or jars, make it easy to prepare Thai-style curries at home; green and red are the most common varieties. Strict vegetarians should be sure to check the label, as some (but not all) varieties contain shrimp paste or fish sauce. **SERVES 4**

2 teaspoons canola or safflower oil

3 tablespoons green curry paste

½ pound shiitake mushrooms, stemmed and halved if large

½ pound green beans, trimmed and halved crosswise

4 heads baby bok choy (about 6 ounces), halved lengthwise

1 red bell pepper, ribs and seeds removed, cut into 1-inch pieces

1 can (13.5 ounces) unsweetened coconut milk

½ cup fresh basil leaves, torn if large

1 In a wok or large skillet, heat oil over medium-high. Add curry paste and cook, stirring, until fragrant, 30 seconds. Add mushrooms, green beans, bok choy, and bell pepper; cook, stirring frequently, until beans are crisp-tender and bright green, about 5 minutes.

2 Add coconut milk and bring just to a simmer (do not let boil). Reduce heat and cook until vegetables are tender, 8 to 10 minutes. To serve, divide among 4 bowls, spoon curry on top, and garnish with basil.

V G S Per serving: 275 calories, 23 g fat (18 g saturated fat), 0 mg cholesterol, 19 g carbohydrates, 5 g protein, 5 g fiber

Marrakesh Stew

An abundance of warming Moroccan spices flavor this early fall stew. Serve it over couscous for a heartier meal. **SERVES 8**

1 tablespoon olive oil

1 large red onion, coarsely chopped

2 teaspoons cumin

1 teaspoon cinnamon

1 teaspoon coriander

½ to 1 teaspoon cayenne

½ teaspoon allspice

4 large carrots, peeled and diced

2 russet potatoes, peeled and diced

1 small butternut squash, peeled, seeded, and diced

Coarse salt and freshly ground pepper

1 can (14½ ounces) diced tomatoes

3¾ cups vegetable stock, preferably homemade (see page 364)

2 small eggplants, cut into 1-inch pieces

1½ cups cooked chickpeas (see page 365), drained and rinsed

Cooked couscous (see page 363), for serving (optional)

1 In an 8-quart Dutch oven or heavy pot, heat olive oil over medium-high. Add onion and cook, stirring occasionally, until soft, about 5 minutes. Add cumin, cinnamon, coriander, cayenne, and allspice and cook, stirring, until fragrant, about 1 minute. Add carrots, potatoes, and squash and season with salt and pepper. Cook, stirring occasionally, until beginning to brown, about 5 minutes.

2 Add tomatoes and stock (vegetables should be completely covered by liquid; add water to cover if necessary). Season with salt and pepper. Bring to a gentle simmer and cook, uncovered, 20 minutes.

3 Add eggplant, stir to combine, and simmer until eggplant is tender, about 20 minutes. Stir in chickpeas, season with salt and pepper, and cook until chickpeas are warmed through, about 5 minutes. Serve with couscous, if desired. (To store, refrigerate cooled stew in an airtight container up to 1 week, or freeze up to 3 months; thaw overnight in refrigerator and reheat over low.)

V G Per serving (without couscous): 212 calories, 3 g fat (0 g saturated fat), 0 mg cholesterol, 44 g carbohydrates, 6 g protein, 9 g fiber

Curried Red Lentil Soup with Dried Cherries and Cilantro

Red lentils provide the base for a vibrant soup that draws from a spectrum of flavors: spicy curry, sweet coconut milk, tart cherries, and fresh cilantro. **SERVES 4**

2 teaspoons canola oil

1 piece (about 2 inches) fresh ginger, peeled and finely chopped

6 garlic cloves, finely chopped (2 tablespoons)

1 large shallot, finely chopped (¼ cup)

2 carrots, peeled and finely diced (about 1 cup)

2 teaspoons curry powder

Coarse salt

¾ cup unsweetened coconut milk

4 cups water

1 cup dried red lentils, picked over and rinsed

⅓ cup coarsely chopped dried cherries

3 tablespoons finely chopped cilantro stems, plus 3 tablespoons cilantro leaves for garnish

1. Heat oil in a medium saucepan over medium. Add ginger, garlic, shallot, and carrots, and cook, stirring often, until softened, about 7 minutes. Add curry powder, and cook, stirring, until fragrant, about 1 minute.

2. Add 1¼ teaspoons salt, ½ cup coconut milk, the water, and lentils, and bring to a boil. Reduce heat, cover, and simmer until lentils and carrots are tender, 8 to 10 minutes. Pass 2 cups soup through a fine sieve into a bowl, reserving solids. Let cool slightly. Working in batches, puree remaining soup with the strained liquid in a blender until smooth, being careful not to fill jar more than halfway each time. Reheat after blending. Stir in reserved solids.

3. Reserving some cherries for garnish, stir cherries and cilantro stems into soup, and ladle into 4 bowls. Dividing evenly, swirl in remaining ¼ cup coconut milk, and garnish with cherries and cilantro leaves. Serve immediately.

🅥🅖🅢 Per serving: 348 calories, 12 g fat (8 g saturated fat), 0 mg cholesterol, 46 g carbohydrates, 15 g protein, 12 g fiber

Creamy Broccoli–White Bean Soup

It's the garnishes—shaved cheese, toasted pine nuts, and a few bright-green broccoli florets—that make this understated vegetable soup feel extra special. **SERVES 4**

1 head broccoli (about 1 pound), cut into florets, stems peeled and thinly sliced

2 tablespoons olive oil

1 onion, diced

2 garlic cloves, thinly sliced

1½ cups cooked cannellini beans (see page 365), drained and rinsed

2½ cups vegetable stock, preferably homemade (see page 364)

Coarse salt and freshly ground pepper

1 tablespoon pine nuts, toasted (see page 363)

Shaved Parmigiano-Reggiano, for garnish

1 Set a steamer basket or colander in a pot filled with 2 inches of boiling water. Add broccoli florets and stems in an even layer. Cover and steam until tender and bright green, about 3 minutes. Let cool slightly. Reserve ½ cup florets for garnish.

2 Heat olive oil in a medium pot over medium. Sauté onion and garlic until translucent, stirring often, about 6 minutes. Add beans and stock and bring mixture to a simmer. Remove from heat and stir in broccoli. Let cool slightly. Working in batches, puree soup in a blender until smooth, being careful not to fill jar more than halfway each time. Reheat after blending. Season with salt and pepper.

3 To serve, divide soup among 4 bowls and garnish with reserved broccoli florets, toasted pine nuts, and shaved cheese.

G Per serving: 247 calories, 10 g fat (2 g saturated fat), 3.12 mg cholesterol, 28 g carbohydrates, 9.97 g protein, 8.24 g fiber

Hearty Winter-Vegetable Soup

Practically any vegetable can go into this soup—indeed, it's a great way to use up whatever you have on hand. **SERVES 10**

4   leeks, white and pale-green parts only

2   tablespoons olive oil

3   celery stalks, chopped

3   carrots, chopped

2   garlic cloves, crushed

2   pinches of crushed red pepper flakes

    Coarse salt and freshly ground pepper

5¼ cups vegetable stock, preferably homemade (see page 364)

1   butternut squash, peeled and diced

2   Yukon Gold potatoes, coarsely chopped

1   head escarole, cut into 1-inch-thick ribbons

1½ cups cooked chickpeas (see page 365), drained and rinsed

2   tablespoons fresh lemon juice

2   tablespoons thinly sliced fresh mint leaves

2   tablespoons thinly sliced fresh dill

1 Halve leeks lengthwise and then cut crosswise into 1-inch pieces. Wash well in several changes of water, then drain.

2 Heat olive oil in a large Dutch oven or heavy pot over medium-high. Cook leeks, celery, carrots, garlic, red pepper flakes, and 1 teaspoon salt, stirring occasionally, until leeks are translucent, about 5 minutes. Add stock and 1½ cups water, and bring to a boil.

3 Add squash and potatoes. Return to a boil. Reduce heat, and simmer, partially covered, until vegetables are tender, about 15 minutes. Stir in escarole and chickpeas, and return to a boil. Stir in lemon juice and herbs. Season with salt and pepper and serve.

V G S Per serving: 172 calories, 3.5 g fat (0.5 g saturated fat), 0 mg cholesterol, 32.85 g carbohydrates, 5.3 g protein, 6.73 g fiber

Chickpea Curry with Roasted Cauliflower and Tomatoes

Toasting the curry powder with other aromatic ingredients before adding the liquid intensifies the flavor of this quick take on *chana masala*. You can roast the cauliflower and tomatoes a couple days ahead; cool, cover, and refrigerate until ready to use. **SERVES 4**

½ head cauliflower (about 1 pound), trimmed and cut into florets

2 tablespoons plus 2 teaspoons extra-virgin olive oil

1½ pints cherry tomatoes

Coarse salt and freshly ground pepper

1 large yellow onion, cut into medium dice

3 garlic cloves, minced

1 tablespoon minced peeled fresh ginger

1 tablespoon plus 1 teaspoon curry powder

3 cups cooked chickpeas (see page 365), drained and rinsed

2½ cups baby spinach

1 tablespoon chopped fresh cilantro leaves

1 Preheat oven to 375°F. Toss cauliflower with 1 teaspoon olive oil and arrange in a single layer on one side of a rimmed baking sheet. Toss tomatoes with 1 teaspoon olive oil and arrange on other side of sheet. Season with salt and pepper. Roast until florets are browned in spots and tomatoes are soft, about 25 minutes.

2 In a medium pot, heat 2 teaspoons oil over medium-high. Cook onion, stirring occasionally, until golden brown, about 10 minutes. Add garlic, ginger, and curry powder and cook, stirring, until fragrant, about 1 minute.

3 Add chickpeas, tomatoes, and 2 cups water; bring to a boil. Reduce heat to medium, cover, and simmer 8 minutes.

4 Add cauliflower and cook until warmed through and chickpeas are tender, about 8 minutes. Stir in spinach and cilantro and season with salt. To serve, divide among 4 bowls (over rice, if desired).

V G S Per serving: 508 calories, 11.56 g fat (1.48 g saturated fat), 0 mg cholesterol, 84.66 g carbohydrates, 17.92 g protein, 13.7 g fiber

Pea and Potato Curry

You can use fresh or frozen peas to make this Indian stew, known as *aloo matar*. Fresh curry leaves—which are actually not related to curry powder—can be found at Indian or Southeast Asian markets and from online retailers. **SERVES 4**

1 teaspoon coriander seeds

1 teaspoon fennel seeds

1 teaspoon mustard seeds

1 tablespoon olive oil

½ cinnamon stick

1 fresh green chile

2 garlic cloves, minced

1 yellow onion, coarsely chopped

1 tablespoon minced peeled fresh ginger

7 fresh curry leaves (optional)

3 large tomatoes, coarsely chopped

1 pound Yukon Gold potatoes, cut into 1-inch pieces

2 cups water

1 cup fresh shelled peas (from 1 pound in pods) or frozen peas (do not thaw)

Coarse salt

2 tablespoons plain Greek-style yogurt

1. Heat a large heavy-bottomed pot over medium. Toast coriander, fennel, and mustard seeds until fragrant, stirring, about 1 minute. Let cool slightly, then process in a spice grinder or clean coffee mill until finely ground. (You can also crush the seeds with the side of a chef's knife.)

2. Heat olive oil in same pot. Add ground seeds, cinnamon, chile, garlic, onion, ginger, and curry leaves (if using). Cook, stirring occasionally, until onion is soft, 6 to 8 minutes. Add tomatoes and bring to a boil, then simmer, stirring occasionally, until slightly thickened, about 15 minutes.

3. Add potatoes and the water. Simmer, partially covered, until potatoes are tender, about 35 minutes. Add fresh peas and cook until tender, about 12 minutes. (If using frozen peas, cook just until heated through, about 5 minutes.) Discard cinnamon stick. Season with salt. Stir in yogurt, and serve.

Ⓖ Per serving: 194 calories, 5 g fat (1 g saturated fat), 1 mg cholesterol, 33 g carbohydrates, 6 g protein, 7 g fiber

Roasted Eggplant and Chickpea Soup

To keep things simple (and minimize cleanup), the eggplant and chickpeas in this recipe are roasted together in the same pan. The finished dish marries the softened eggplant and crunchy chickpeas for a thick and chunky soup with lots of textural contrast. **SERVES 4**

2 eggplants (about 1½ pounds total), peeled and cut into 1-inch pieces

1 small yellow onion, diced medium

2 garlic cloves, unpeeled

2 tablespoons olive oil

Coarse salt and freshly ground pepper

1½ cups cooked chickpeas (see page 365), drained and rinsed, patted dry

4 cups vegetable stock, preferably homemade (see page 364), or water

Fresh oregano leaves, for serving (optional)

Plain low-fat yogurt, for serving (optional)

1 Preheat oven to 400°F. In a large bowl, toss together eggplant, onion, garlic, and 1 tablespoon plus 1 teaspoon olive oil; season with salt and pepper. Arrange in a single layer on a rimmed baking sheet, leaving empty space at one end. In same bowl, toss chickpeas with remaining 2 teaspoons oil. Transfer to empty space on sheet.

2 Roast until eggplant is golden and cooked through and chickpeas are slightly crunchy, about 35 minutes. When cool enough to handle, peel garlic.

3 In a medium pot, combine garlic, eggplant, onion, and stock or water. Bring mixture to a simmer over medium-high heat. With a potato masher or the back of a wooden spoon, mash some eggplant until soup is thick and chunky. Stir in chickpeas and season with salt and pepper. To serve, divide among 4 bowls and top with oregano and yogurt as desired.

G Per serving: 309 calories, 10.2 g fat (1.3 g saturated fat), 0 mg cholesterol, 43.1 g carbohydrates, 14.8 g protein, 14.5 g fiber

Cavolo Nero and Cannellini Bean Soup

Winter calls for robust flavors as well as for foods that are substantial and nourishing. This hearty Italian soup, which pairs bitter greens with buttery white beans, satisfies on both counts. **SERVES 6**

1½ pounds Lacinato (Tuscan) kale, tough stems removed, coarsely chopped

Coarse salt and freshly ground pepper

2 tablespoons olive oil

⅓ cup finely chopped red onion

3 garlic cloves, thinly sliced

1 dried red chile, such as chile de árbol, crumbled

½ teaspoon fennel seeds

5 cups vegetable stock, preferably homemade (see page 364)

8 ounces dried cannellini beans, soaked (see page 365)

1 tomato, seeded and finely chopped

¼ loaf Tuscan bread (about 6 ounces), cut into ½-inch-thick slices and toasted

1 Prepare an ice-water bath. Blanch kale in a large saucepan of boiling salted water until just tender, 3 to 5 minutes. Drain, reserving ¼ cup cooking liquid. Transfer kale to ice bath to stop the cooking; drain.

2 Heat olive oil in a large saucepan over medium. Add onion; cook, stirring occasionally, until tender, about 5 minutes. Add garlic, chile, and fennel seeds; cook, stirring occasionally, 2 minutes.

3 Stir in stock, beans, and tomato. Bring to a boil. Reduce to a simmer, and cook, stirring occasionally, until beans are tender, about 45 minutes.

4 Add kale and reserved cooking liquid. Season with salt and pepper. Cook, stirring, until kale is warmed through and very tender, about 5 minutes. To serve, divide bread and soup among 4 bowls.

V Per serving: 290 calories, 7 g fat (1 g saturated fat), 1 mg cholesterol, 47 g carbohydrates, 13 g protein, 4 g fiber

Roasted-Vegetable Ratatouille

This Provençal dish is an easy and economical celebration of seasonal vegetables stewed with garlic and olive oil. Try it over barley or polenta, topped with a poached egg, or simply spooned over grilled or toasted crusty bread. **SERVES 6**

1 large eggplant, cut into 1-inch pieces

4 medium zucchini, cut into 1-inch pieces

½ cup plus 2 tablespoons extra-virgin olive oil

2 tablespoons coarsely chopped fresh thyme

Coarse salt and freshly ground pepper

4 garlic cloves, minced

2 onions, halved and cut into half-moons

6 pounds tomatoes, peeled (see page 364) and cut into quarters, seeds discarded

2 bell peppers (1 red and 1 yellow), roasted (see page 364) and sliced lengthwise into ½-inch-thick strips

½ cup coarsely chopped fresh basil

½ cup coarsely chopped fresh flat-leaf parsley

1 Preheat oven to 400°F. Toss eggplant, zucchini, ½ cup oil, and 1 tablespoon thyme on a large rimmed baking sheet. Season with salt and pepper and spread in an even layer. Roast, tossing occasionally, until golden, about 1 hour.

2 Heat remaining 2 tablespoons oil in a large, deep skillet over medium-high. Add garlic and onions; cook, stirring frequently, until soft, about 4 minutes. Add tomatoes and peppers; cook until tomatoes are soft, about 7 minutes.

3 Add eggplant and zucchini, ¼ cup basil, and remaining tablespoon thyme. Season with salt and pepper. Reduce heat to medium-low; simmer, stirring occasionally, until vegetables are very soft, about 30 minutes. Stir in parsley and remaining ¼ cup basil. Cook just until heated through, about 1 minute more. Serve hot or at room temperature.

V G S Per serving: 370 calories, 24.91 g fat (3.53 g saturated fat), 0 mg cholesterol, 35.52 g carbohydrates, 7.85 g protein, 12.44 g fiber

Roasted Beet-Garlic Soup

Roasting the beets and garlic before adding them to the pot enhances their natural sweetness, so very little else is needed to give this beautifully hued soup its deep flavor. Once roasted, the beet skins are easy to rub off. **SERVES 4**

3 medium beets (about 12 ounces)

2 tablespoons extra-virgin olive oil, plus more for drizzling

6 garlic cloves (unpeeled)

1 leek, white and pale-green parts only, thinly sliced, washed well, and drained

1 teaspoon fresh thyme leaves

1 bay leaf

3 cups water

Coarse salt and freshly ground pepper

2 tablespoons fresh lemon juice

1 Preheat oven to 400°F. Drizzle beets with olive oil and wrap in parchment, then foil; roast until tender when pierced with a sharp knife, about 1 hour. Meanwhile, drizzle garlic cloves with oil and roast in a separate parchment-foil packet until tender, about 30 minutes. Let cool slightly, then peel beets with paper towels and quarter. Squeeze garlic cloves from papery skins.

2 Heat 2 tablespoons olive oil in a medium pot over medium. Add leek and cook, stirring, until tender, 6 to 8 minutes. Add beets, garlic, thyme, bay leaf, and the water. Season with salt and pepper.

3 Bring to a boil; reduce heat and simmer 5 minutes. Discard bay leaf. Let cool slightly. Working in batches, puree soup in a blender until smooth, being careful not to fill jar more than halfway each time. Reheat after blending. Stir in lemon juice and season with salt and pepper before serving.

V G S Per serving: 130 calories, 9 g fat (1 g saturated fat), 0 mg cholesterol, 11.36 g carbohydrates, 2 g protein, 3 g fiber

Spiced Butternut Squash Soup

One of the easiest soups to prepare and a nearly universal favorite (especially for Thanksgiving), butternut squash soup takes well to experimentation. This version incorporates a blend of classic seasonings that includes fresh ginger in addition to cinnamon, cardamom, and cloves, but you can vary the spices or replace them with fresh herbs such as sage or rosemary. **SERVES 6**

- 2 tablespoons olive oil
- 1 onion, chopped
- 2 garlic cloves, chopped
- 2 tablespoons grated peeled fresh ginger
- ½ teaspoon ground turmeric
- ⅛ teaspoon ground cinnamon
- ⅛ teaspoon ground cardamom
- Dash of ground cloves
- 2 carrots, peeled and chopped
- 1 tart apple, peeled, quartered, and chopped
- 4 cups peeled, seeded, and chopped butternut squash (from 1 large squash)
- 3 cups water
- Coarse salt and freshly ground pepper

1 Heat olive oil in a medium saucepan over medium. Add onion and garlic and cook, stirring often, until tender, 6 to 8 minutes. Add ginger, turmeric, cinnamon, cardamom, and cloves and cook until fragrant, about 1 minute.

2 Add carrots, apple, butternut squash, and the water. Bring to a boil; cover partially and reduce to a simmer. Season with salt and pepper. Cook until vegetables are tender, about 20 minutes.

3 Let cool slightly. Working in batches, puree soup in a blender until smooth, being careful not to fill jar more than halfway each time. Reheat after blending, then season with salt and pepper. Serve sprinkled with more pepper.

V G S Per serving: 147 calories, 5 g fat (1 g saturated fat), 0 mg cholesterol, 26.38 g carbohydrates, 2 g protein, 5 g fiber

VERSATILE VEGETARIAN:
CHILI

A bowl of chili is a tried-and-true vegetarian main course, and with good reason: it's hearty but not heavy, packed with protein, and highly adaptable. There's an infinite number of ways to vary the basic recipe below, including a bevy of toppings (see page 148) for a build-it-yourself buffet.

SAUTÉ AROMATICS   TOAST SEASONINGS   ADD BEANS AND SIMMER

VEGETARIAN BEAN CHILI SERVES 6

2 tablespoons olive oil

1 large onion, chopped

1 poblano chile, ribs and seeds removed, chopped

4 garlic cloves, minced

Coarse salt

1 can (4 ounces) diced green chiles

1 tablespoon plus 1½ teaspoons chili powder

2 teaspoons ground cumin

3 cups cooked kidney beans (see page 365), drained and rinsed

3 cups cooked pinto beans (see page 365), drained and rinsed

1 can (28 ounces) diced tomatoes, with juice

Assorted toppings, for serving

1. In a large Dutch oven or other heavy pot, heat olive oil over medium-high. Add onion, poblano, and garlic; season with salt. Cook, stirring occasionally, until onion is translucent, about 4 minutes.

2. Stir in green chiles, chili powder, and cumin; cook, stirring frequently, until spices are darkened and fragrant, about 3 minutes.

3. Add beans, tomatoes and their juice, and 2 cups water; bring to a boil over high heat. Reduce to a simmer and cook until vegetables are tender and chili is thickened, 20 to 30 minutes.

4. Remove from the heat. Season with salt. Serve with suggested toppings (see page 148), as desired.

G Per serving (without toppings): 342 calories, 7 g fat (1 g saturated fat), 0 mg cholesterol, 57 g carbohydrates, 17 g protein, 18 g fiber

TOASTED PEPITAS

SLICED SCALLIONS

YOGURT

CHOPPED CILANTRO

TOASTED TORTILLA STRIPS

DICED TOMATO

DICED ONION

GRATED CHEESE

SLICED AVOCADO

LIME WEDGES

FRESH CORN KERNELS

TOP IT OFF

Chili actually benefits from a little improvisation, and assorted toppings are a good way to change up the flavor and texture. In many cases the toppings can temper the heat as well. Choose among those shown opposite. See page 363 for how to toast pepitas. Toast whole flour or corn tortillas over the flame of a gas burner, turning with tongs, until lightly charred, about 30 seconds per side; let cool slightly and cut into strips. Try queso blanco or Monterey Jack cheese.

VARY THE BEANS

Swap in an equal amount of other beans: in addition to the pinto and kidney beans used in the master recipe (page 146), black, navy, and pink beans are all common in chili; black-eyed peas, chickpeas, or lentils would also work. Use just one type of bean or a combination of two or three. Just make sure to keep the total volume the same.

ADD SEASONAL VEGETABLES

Practically any vegetable can be added to chili; usually it will be cooked along with the onion and chile until tender, before the other ingredients are added. For a summer version, add up to 1 cup diced red, yellow, or green bell peppers (or a mix); sliced zucchini or yellow squash; or fresh corn kernels, alone or in combination. For an autumn chili, add up to 1 cup peeled, diced butternut squash or sweet potato; chopped Swiss chard, kale, or other sturdy greens; or diced mushrooms.

MAKE IT GREEN

Puree 3 pounds tomatillos, husked and washed, until smooth in a food processor or blender. Use this puree in place of the canned tomatoes in the master recipe.

INCREASE THE HEAT

Add 1 to 2 tablespoons minced fresh green chile, such as jalapeño or serrano. (As a general rule, the smaller the chile, the hotter it is.) Or try adding 1 to 2 tablespoons minced canned chipotle chile in adobo sauce to impart a smoky flavor.

MAXIMIZE THE FLAVORS

Broil the vegetables for deeper flavor: Before getting started, halve the onion and poblano chile, and place cut side down on a baking sheet; add whole (peeled) garlic cloves and broil until just starting to char, then chop and sauté as directed. You could also broil a pound of fresh plum tomatoes, halved lengthwise, until softened and starting to char, then dice or puree in a blender; use this puree in place of the canned tomatoes.

casseroles and other baked dishes

Lighter Macaroni and Cheese

A good recipe for mac and cheese should be in every home cook's regular rotation, especially those who frequently find themselves cooking for both vegetarians and meat-eaters. Make this more healthful version in a large baking dish as shown on page 150, or in single-serve ramekins (see opposite). **SERVES 8**

6   small (3-inch) vine-ripened tomatoes, each cut into four ¼-inch-thick slices (24 slices total)

3   tablespoons olive oil

1½ teaspoons fresh thyme leaves, plus sprigs for garnish

Coarse salt and freshly ground pepper

5   slices whole wheat sandwich bread

2   tablespoons unsalted butter

16 ounces elbow macaroni

2   cups vegetable stock, preferably homemade (see page 364)

5   tablespoons all-purpose flour

Pinch of freshly grated nutmeg

Pinch of cayenne pepper

2   cups low-fat milk

8   ounces extra-sharp cheddar, grated (about 2¼ cups)

1   ounce Parmigiano-Reggiano, finely grated (about ¼ cup)

1 Preheat oven to 400°F. Arrange tomatoes in a single layer on 2 rimmed baking sheets. Drizzle each batch with 1 tablespoon olive oil; sprinkle each batch with ½ teaspoon thyme, and season with salt and pepper. Bake until tomatoes have softened, about 20 minutes. (Leave oven on.)

2 Process bread in a food processor until coarse crumbs form. Melt 1 tablespoon butter with remaining tablespoon olive oil in a medium skillet over medium heat. Add bread crumbs, and toss to coat. Season with salt and pepper.

3 Cook pasta in a pot of boiling salted water 2 to 3 minutes less than package directions. Drain in a colander and run under cold water to stop the cooking; drain again. Transfer to a large bowl.

4 Whisk ½ cup stock into the flour in a medium bowl. Melt remaining tablespoon butter in a medium saucepan over medium heat. Stir in nutmeg, cayenne, remaining ½ teaspoon thyme, and 1 teaspoon salt. Add milk and remaining 1½ cups stock. Whisk in flour mixture. Bring to a boil, whisking frequently. Reduce to a simmer. Cook 8 minutes, whisking frequently. Add both cheeses; cook, stirring, until melted. Pour over macaroni, stirring to combine.

5 Arrange half the tomato slices in the bottom of a 2-quart shallow baking dish, add macaroni mixture, then top with remaining tomato slices. (Alternatively, put 2 tomato slices in the bottom of each of eight 4½-by-1¼-inch ramekins. Divide macaroni mixture evenly among ramekins and top each with a tomato slice.) Sprinkle with bread crumbs and thyme sprigs. Bake until bubbling and golden brown, about 30 minutes. Let cool slightly before serving.

Per serving: 530 calories, 21.23 g fat (10.87 g saturated fat), 43.47 mg cholesterol, 63.29 g carbohydrates, 19.9 g protein, 3.88 g fiber

Zucchini-Ribbon "Lasagna"

Strips of zucchini stand in for noodles to make this gluten-free lasagna. Crumbled tofu adds protein to the tomato sauce; ricotta is dolloped on top (and in each layer) before baking. **SERVES 9**

FOR THE SAUCE

1 can (28 ounces) whole peeled plum tomatoes, with juice

2 tablespoons olive oil

1 small onion, finely chopped

¼ teaspoon crushed red pepper flakes

12 ounces firm tofu, drained and pressed (see page 363)

2 tablespoons chopped fresh oregano leaves

Coarse salt

FOR THE LASAGNA

2 zucchini (about 1 pound total), ends trimmed

1 cup (8 ounces) part-skim ricotta cheese

¼ teaspoon olive oil

Freshly ground pepper

1 Make the sauce: Pulse tomatoes with their juice in a food processor until finely chopped. Heat olive oil in a large straight-sided skillet over medium. Cook onion and red pepper flakes, stirring occasionally, until onion is softened, about 8 minutes. Add tomatoes; bring to a boil. Reduce heat and simmer until thickened, about 20 minutes. Coarsely crumble tofu and stir into sauce with chopped oregano; season with salt. Let cool.

2 Make the lasagna: Preheat oven to 375°F. Slice zucchini lengthwise into thin strips (about ⅛ inch thick) using a mandoline or a sharp knife. Place 5 or 6 zucchini slices, overlapping slightly, in the bottom of an 8-inch square baking dish. Top with 1 cup sauce. Dot evenly with ¼ cup cheese. Repeat twice with zucchini, remaining sauce, and ½ cup cheese. Top with remaining zucchini; brush with the olive oil. Dot with remaining ¼ cup cheese, and season with pepper. Bake, uncovered, until lasagna bubbles and top browns, 50 to 60 minutes. Let stand 10 minutes before serving.

G Per serving: 128 calories, 7.75 g fat (2.03 g saturated fat), 8.54 mg cholesterol, 8.46 g carbohydrates, 8.26 g protein, 1.73 g fiber

Apple, Leek, and Squash Gratin

Apples may seem an unlikely addition to a savory gratin, but here slices of the fruit arranged on top provide another layer (literally) of flavor. Butternut squash is what gives this main course its staying power; other types of squash, such as delicata or kabocha, are fine substitutes. **SERVES 4**

3 tablespoons olive oil

2 leeks, white part only, thinly sliced crosswise, washed well and drained

2 tablespoons water

Coarse salt and freshly ground pepper

½ cup dry sherry

1 tablespoon chopped fresh sage leaves, plus whole leaves for garnish

1 pound butternut squash, peeled, seeded, and cut into ⅛-inch-thick slices

1 pound apples, such as Gala, Cortland, Baldwin, or Macoun, peeled, halved, cored, and cut into ⅛-inch-thick slices

2 ounces finely grated Parmigiano-Reggiano (½ cup)

1 Preheat oven to 350°F. In a 10-inch skillet, heat 2 tablespoons olive oil over medium. Add leeks and the water; season with salt and pepper. Cook, stirring occasionally, until leeks begin to brown, about 10 minutes. Add sherry and sage and cook, stirring, until liquid is reduced to a glaze, about 3 minutes.

2 In a 2-quart shallow baking dish, arrange squash in overlapping layers; season with salt and pepper. Spread leeks evenly over the squash. Arrange apples in an overlapping layer over the leeks. Brush apples with remaining tablespoon oil. Cover tightly with parchment, then foil. Bake 45 minutes.

3 Uncover and sprinkle cheese over the top. Raise oven temperature to 450°F. Continue baking until the cheese has melted and is golden brown, about 10 minutes more. Let cool 10 minutes before serving, garnished with sage leaves.

G Per serving: 264 calories, 13 g fat (3.92 g saturated fat), 12.47 mg cholesterol, 30 g carbohydrates, 6 g protein, 5 g fiber

Vegetable-Barley Potpies

Filled with a hearty mix of mushrooms, barley, and white beans, these potpies are just as satisfying as more traditional chicken versions. Phyllo dough offers a quicker—and delectably flaky—alternative to a pâté brisée top. **MAKES 4**

2 tablespoons extra-virgin olive oil, plus more for brushing

1 onion, finely diced

2 carrots, thinly sliced

4 ounces shiitake mushrooms, stemmed and thinly sliced

¼ cup dry white wine

1½ cups cooked pearl barley (see page 371)

2 cups cooked white beans (see page 365), drained and rinsed

2 tablespoons all-purpose flour

4 cups vegetable stock, preferably homemade (see page 364)

2 tablespoons chopped fresh flat-leaf parsley, plus more for garnish

6 sheets frozen phyllo dough, preferably whole wheat, thawed

Sea salt, for sprinkling

1 Heat olive oil in a large skillet over medium. Sauté onion, carrots, and mushrooms until tender, stirring frequently, 6 to 8 minutes. Add wine; cook, stirring up browned bits, until almost all the wine has evaporated.

2 Combine barley and beans in a large pot. Whisk flour into stock and add to pot. Bring to a boil and cook, stirring, until slightly thickened. Remove from heat. Stir in parsley and let cool slightly.

3 Preheat oven to 425°F. Using a 12-ounce ramekin as a guide, cut out 4 rounds from phyllo; keep covered with a damp paper towel. Spoon barley mixture into 4 ramekins. Brush each cut sheet with oil and place on top of filled ramekin. Cut vents into tops. Sprinkle with sea salt and reserved parsley.

4 Transfer to a rimmed baking sheet and bake until tops are golden and filling is bubbling, about 30 minutes. Let cool slightly before serving.

V Per serving: 492 calories, 11.9 g fat (1.93 g saturated fat), 0 mg cholesterol, 78.25 g carbohydrates, 17.22 g protein, 13.62 g fiber

Sweet Potato and Cauliflower Gratin

An optional garnish of fried sage leaves takes this rustic gratin from simple to spectacular. **SERVES 6**

2 tablespoons olive oil

3 tablespoons all-purpose flour

1 cup whole milk

1 cup water

¼ cup plus 1 tablespoon finely grated Parmigiano-Reggiano (about 1 ounce)

1 tablespoon chopped fresh sage leaves, plus whole leaves for garnish (optional)

Coarse salt and freshly ground pepper

2 pounds sweet potatoes, peeled and sliced ¼ inch thick

1 head cauliflower, trimmed, quartered, and sliced ¼ inch thick

Canola oil, for crisping sage (optional)

1 Preheat oven to 350°F. Heat olive oil in a pot over medium. Add flour and cook, stirring, 1 minute. Slowly whisk in milk and the water. Cook, whisking, until thickened, about 12 minutes. Remove from heat; stir in ¼ cup cheese and the chopped sage. Season with salt and pepper.

2 Pour one-third of sauce in bottom of a 3-quart shallow baking dish. Arrange a third of the sweet potato and cauliflower in an overlapping layer, alternating vegetables. Season with salt and pepper. Repeat twice with remaining sauce and vegetables. Cover with parchment, then foil; bake until tender, about 1 hour.

3 Raise oven temperature to 425°F. Uncover and sprinkle with remaining cheese. Bake until golden brown, about 20 minutes. Let stand 10 minutes.

4 Meanwhile, if desired, heat 1 inch canola oil in a small pot over medium-high until shimmering. Cook a few sage leaves at a time until crisp, about 10 seconds. Transfer to a paper towel to drain. Season with salt. Sprinkle leaves onto gratin and serve.

Per serving: 208 calories, 9 g fat (2 g saturated fat), 6 mg cholesterol, 28 g carbohydrates, 5 g protein, 5 g fiber

Farro Pasta and Mushroom Gratin

Farro pasta offers more fiber than semolina pasta and a nutty flavor that pairs well with the goat cheese in this dish. **SERVES 6**

1 package (17.6 ounces) farro pasta such as strozzapreti, gemelli, or penne

Coarse salt and freshly ground pepper

3 slices multi-grain sandwich bread

3½ cups skim milk

¼ cup all-purpose flour

1½ teaspoons finely chopped fresh sage leaves

1 log (5½ ounces) fresh goat cheese

Canola or safflower oil, for dish

8 ounces portobello mushrooms, very thinly sliced (about 4½ cups)

1. Cook pasta in a pot of boiling salted water 2 to 3 minutes less than package instructions; drain. Pulse bread in a food processor until coarse crumbs form.

2. Preheat oven to 375°F. Whisk together milk, flour, sage, 1½ teaspoons salt, and ¼ teaspoon pepper in a saucepan. Bring to a boil, whisking often. Add half the cheese; cook, whisking, until thickened, 2 minutes. Remove from heat.

3. Lightly coat a 2-quart baking dish with oil. Toss mushrooms, pasta, and cheese mixture in a bowl; transfer to baking dish. Crumble remaining cheese on top and sprinkle with bread crumbs. Cover dish with parchment, then foil. Bake until mushrooms are tender, 25 to 30 minutes. Uncover and continue baking until crumbs are browned, about 7 minutes more. Let cool 5 minutes before serving.

Per serving: 473 calories, 6 g fat (4 g saturated fat), 15 mg cholesterol, 73 g carbohydrates, 24 g protein, 10 g fiber

Italian Baked Eggplant with Seitan

Seitan (pronounced SAY-tan), a hearty meat substitute made from wheat gluten, is widely used in Asian stir-fries and soups as a protein-rich addition. Like tofu, it has a mild taste that readily absorbs other flavors. Here, slices of seitan are coated with bread crumbs and nutritional yeast—an inactive form of yeast with a flavor similar to cheese—and sautéed until golden, then layered with eggplant, spinach, and tomato sauce in a vegan casserole. Look for nutritional yeast at health-food stores, where it is often sold in bulk. **SERVES 6**

  1 eggplant, sliced crosswise ¼ inch thick
    Coarse salt and freshly ground pepper
  ½ cup olive oil, plus more if needed
  ½ small onion, finely chopped
  3 garlic cloves, minced
  1 can (28 ounces) whole tomatoes with juice, pulsed
    fine in a food processor
  1 tablespoon chopped fresh oregano leaves
1½ cups whole-wheat bread crumbs
  2 teaspoons nutritional yeast
  8 ounces store-bought or homemade seitan (see
    page 366), drained and thinly sliced
  ½ cup soy or other non-dairy milk
  2 tablespoons whole ground flaxseed meal
  2 cups fresh baby spinach (2 ounces)

1 Sprinkle eggplant slices generously with salt and let drain in a colander, about 30 minutes. Rinse well with water, drain, and pat dry.

2 Meanwhile, heat 2 tablespoons olive oil in a medium saucepan over medium. Cook onion and garlic, stirring, until translucent, about 6 minutes. Add tomatoes. Bring mixture to a boil; reduce heat and simmer, stirring occasionally, until sauce is slightly reduced, about 20 minutes. Remove from heat and stir in oregano.

3 Preheat oven to 350°F. In a shallow dish, mix bread crumbs and nutritional yeast; season with salt and pepper. Coat both sides of seitan slices in the mixture, shaking off excess bread crumbs. Heat 2 tablespoons oil in a large skillet over medium. Cook seitan in a single layer until golden brown, about 6 minutes per side. Transfer to a plate and wipe pan clean.

4 Meanwhile, stir together soy milk and flaxseed meal in a shallow dish. Dip eggplant in meal mixture, drain, and coat each piece with bread-crumb mixture, pressing to coat both sides and shaking off excess crumbs. Heat 2 tablespoons oil over medium in same pan. Cook half the eggplant in a single layer until golden brown, adding more oil as necessary, about 6 minutes per side. Transfer to a plate. Wipe pan clean and repeat with remaining eggplant, adding more oil.

5 Spread 1 cup tomato sauce evenly in a 9-by-13-inch baking dish. Arrange half the eggplant on top, slightly overlapping slices, then layer with seitan, spinach, and remaining sauce, and top with remaining eggplant. Cover with parchment, then foil, and bake until bubbling, abut 50 minutes. Uncover and bake until golden brown on top, about 10 minutes more. Let rest 10 minutes before serving.

V Per serving: 409 calories, 21.9 g fat (3.23 g saturated fat), 0 mg cholesterol, 37.77 g carbohydrates, 18.32 g protein, 8.16 g fiber

Cheese Enchilada Casserole

The sauce for this Tex-Mex favorite comes together quickly in a blender and requires brief heating just to thicken; make it up to a few days ahead and refrigerate until you are ready to assemble the casserole. And don't forget to include all the usual toppings, which are an essential part of the dish's appeal. **SERVES 4**

1½ cups Tomato-Jalapeño Enchilada Sauce (page 368)

8 corn tortillas (6-inch size)

2 cups shredded or crumbled cheese, such as Monterey Jack or queso fresco, or a combination

Assorted garnishes such as diced onion, sliced avocado, chopped fresh cilantro leaves, grated cheese, and sour cream, for serving

1 Preheat oven to 350°F. Pour 1 cup sauce into a wide, shallow bowl. Working with one at a time, dip tortillas in sauce, shake off excess, then place on a clean work surface and sprinkle ¼ cup cheese down center.

2 Roll tortilla around cheese and arrange, seam side down, in an 8-inch square baking dish. Once all tortillas have been filled and rolled, top with remaining ½ cup sauce.

3 Cover tightly with parchment, then foil, and bake until heated through, about 10 minutes. Serve with assorted garnishes, as desired.

Ⓖ Per serving (without garnishes): 379 calories, 20.94 g fat (11.15 g saturated fat), 50.29 mg cholesterol, 31.98 g carbohydrates, 18.13 g protein, 4.48 g fiber

Butternut Squash Baked Risotto

The beauty of baked risotto—as opposed to stovetop versions—lies in its ease. What makes this one particularly appealing (and substantial) is the unusually high vegetable-to-rice ratio, thanks to liberal amounts of kale and butternut squash. **SERVES 4**

2 tablespoons olive oil

2 shallots, finely chopped

2 garlic cloves, minced

1 teaspoon fresh thyme leaves

1½ cups Arborio rice

Coarse salt and freshly ground pepper

½ cup dry white wine

1 butternut squash (2 pounds), peeled and cut into medium dice (4 cups)

4 cups vegetable stock, preferably homemade (see page 364)

1 bunch Lacinato (Tuscan) or curly kale, tough stems removed, cut crosswise into ½-inch-thick strips

Grated Parmigiano-Reggiano, for serving

1 Preheat oven to 400°F. In a medium Dutch oven or other heavy ovenproof pot, heat olive oil over medium-high. Add shallots and cook, stirring occasionally, until soft, about 3 minutes. Add garlic and thyme and cook, stirring, until fragrant, about 1 minute.

2 Add rice and cook, stirring frequently, until edges are translucent, about 3 minutes; season with salt and pepper. Add wine and cook, stirring, until completely absorbed, about 2 minutes. Add squash and stock; bring mixture to a boil. Stir in kale.

3 Cover with lid (or with parchment, then foil); transfer to oven, and bake until rice is tender and has absorbed most of the liquid, about 20 minutes. Serve hot, sprinkled with cheese.

Ⓖ Per serving: 383 calories, 7.8 g fat (1.1 g saturated fat), 4.4 mg cholesterol, 73.7 g carbohydrates, 7.8 g protein, 6.8 g fiber

Mini Broccoli and Pasta Casseroles

Comfort food, reconsidered: less pasta, a lighter sauce, more broccoli (even the stems are included), and whole-wheat bread crumbs add up to a much more wholesome dish. **MAKES 6**

2 slices whole-wheat sandwich bread

1 head broccoli (about 1 pound), cut into florets, stems peeled and cut into ½-inch pieces

Coarse salt and freshly ground pepper

8 ounces whole-wheat fusilli pasta

1 tablespoon plus 1 teaspoon olive oil

1 onion, finely chopped

3 tablespoons plus 1½ teaspoons all-purpose flour

1 teaspoon ground mustard

4 cups skim milk

¼ cup part-skim ricotta cheese, pureed in a food processor

4 ounces finely grated Parmigiano-Reggiano (1 cup)

1. Preheat oven to 425°F. Pulse bread in a food processor until fine crumbs form. Transfer to a baking sheet and toast 8 minutes, tossing halfway through.

2. Cook broccoli in a large pot of boiling salted water until slightly tender, about 2 minutes. Transfer to a bowl using a slotted spoon. Add pasta to pot, and cook 2 to 3 minutes less than package instructions. Drain.

3. Wipe pot clean. Add olive oil and heat over medium. Sauté onion, stirring, until translucent, about 7 minutes. Add flour and ground mustard. Cook, stirring, 1 minute. Whisk in milk in a slow, steady stream. Bring to a boil. Cook, whisking, until thickened, about 5 minutes. Remove from heat. Add cheeses and season with salt and pepper.

4. Stir broccoli and pasta into sauce. Divide mixture among six 1½-cup baking dishes; top with bread crumbs. Bake on a rimmed baking sheet until bubbling and tops are browned, 25 to 30 minutes. Let cool slightly before serving.

Per serving: 337 calories, 7 g fat (3 g saturated fat), 16 mg cholesterol, 49 g carbohydrates, 18 g protein, 6 g fiber

Black-Bean Tortilla Casserole

Budin Azteca, a Mexican specialty, is usually made with chicken, yet it's just as rich and delicious with a meat-free—in this case, black-bean and spinach—filling. To prepare (and eat) it is to appreciate why the dish is also known as "Mexican lasagna": softened corn tortillas are layered with a savory filling, grated cheese, and sauce, then baked until golden and bubbling. **SERVES 8**

4 fresh poblano chiles, roasted (see page 364)

18 corn tortillas (6-inch size), halved

¼ cup plus 3 tablespoons canola or safflower oil

10 ounces spinach, tough stems removed

Coarse salt

1 small onion, thinly sliced

4 garlic cloves, minced

3 cups cooked black beans (see page 365), drained and rinsed

1 cup Mexican crema or sour cream, plus more for serving

2¼ cups store-bought or homemade tomatillo salsa (see page 368), plus more for serving

1½ cups (8 ounces) grated queso fresco or Monterey Jack, or a combination

1 Remove and discard stems, seeds, and ribs from roasted chiles; cut chiles into 1-by-½-inch strips. Transfer to a nonreactive bowl.

2 Preheat oven to 425°F. Brush tortilla halves on both sides with 3 tablespoons oil, dividing evenly. Arrange on baking sheets. Bake, rotating sheets halfway through, until tortillas begin to bubble (but are not yet crisp), 5 to 7 minutes. Reduce oven temperature to 350°F.

3 Wash spinach, then drain but leave water clinging to leaves. Heat a large skillet over medium. Add spinach; cover, and cook until wilted, about 2 minutes. Season with salt. Transfer to a colander; let cool slightly, then squeeze out excess moisture. Coarsely chop spinach.

4 Heat 2 tablespoons oil in a medium skillet over medium. Add onion and season with salt; cook, stirring occasionally, until translucent, about 3 minutes. Stir in chiles; cook until heated through, about 1 minute. Transfer to a bowl.

5 Heat remaining 2 tablespoons oil in same skillet. Cook garlic, stirring, 30 seconds. Add beans and season with salt; cook, mashing slightly with the back of a wooden spoon, 2 minutes. Transfer to a separate bowl.

6 Line bottom of a 10¼-inch-round, 2½- to 3-inch-deep baking dish with 12 tortilla halves, overlapping slightly. Layer with chile mixture, half the bean mixture, and half the crema. Spread ¾ cup salsa over top. Sprinkle with ½ cup cheese. Repeat for second layer, using spinach instead of the chiles. Top with remaining tortillas, ¾ cup salsa, and ½ cup cheese.

7 Bake until heated through, 45 minutes to 1 hour; cover with parchment, then foil, for last 15 minutes if browning too quickly or becoming too dry. Let stand 15 minutes before serving, with additional salsa and crema.

Ⓖ Per serving: 549 calories, 29.47 g fat (10.27 g saturated fat), 37.88 mg cholesterol, 54.4 g carbohydrates, 19.53 g protein, 12.28 g fiber

Portobello Gratins

Portobello mushroom caps, a vegetarian staple, are the perfect size and shape for filling and baking into single-serving "gratins." **MAKES 6**

2 tablespoons olive oil, plus more for baking sheet

6 portobello mushrooms, stems removed and reserved

1 ounce finely grated Parmigiano-Reggiano (¼ cup)

¼ cup plain dry bread crumbs

3 tablespoons finely chopped fresh flat-leaf parsley leaves

3 tablespoons snipped fresh chives

2 shallots, thinly sliced

1 pound white or cremini mushrooms, thinly sliced

½ cup dry white wine

½ cup heavy cream

Coarse salt and freshly ground pepper

1 Preheat oven to 350°F. Lightly oil a rimmed baking sheet. Arrange portobello caps, gill sides down, on sheet. Bake until tender, 20 to 25 minutes. Transfer to a plate to cool. Heat broiler, with rack 6 inches from the heat source.

2 Stir together cheese, bread crumbs, 1 tablespoon parsley, 1 tablespoon chives, and 1 tablespoon oil.

3 Chop portobello stems into ½-inch pieces. Heat remaining tablespoon oil in a large skillet over medium until hot but not smoking. Add shallots; cook, stirring, until softened, about 2 minutes. Add sliced mushrooms and chopped stems; cook, stirring occasionally, until tender, 6 to 7 minutes. Add wine; cook until most of the liquid has evaporated, about 2 minutes. Stir in cream and remaining parsley and chives, and season with salt and pepper. Remove from heat.

4 Arrange caps, gill sides up, on a clean baking sheet. Divide mushroom mixture and then crumb mixture among caps. Broil until bubbling and golden brown, about 2 minutes. Serve immediately.

Per serving: 232 calories, 13.95 g fat (6.11 g saturated fat), 31.33 mg cholesterol, 17.33 g carbohydrates, 8.96 g protein, 3.15 g fiber

Herbed Ricotta Soufflé

The French classic—and dinner-party standard—lightens up with fresh ricotta providing the creaminess in place of the traditional béchamel sauce. Room-temperature egg whites will achieve the most volume; beat them by hand with a balloon whisk or use a mixer with a whisk attachment. **SERVES 4**

Unsalted butter, for coating dish

All-purpose flour, for coating dish

1½ cups part-skim ricotta

4 large eggs, separated, room temperature

Coarse salt and freshly ground pepper

2 tablespoons chopped fresh basil leaves

2 tablespoons minced fresh chives

1 Preheat oven to 375°F, with rack in lower third. Butter a 1-quart casserole dish and dust with flour, shaking out excess. Whisk together ricotta, egg yolks, ½ teaspoon salt, and the herbs in a medium bowl; season with pepper. In a separate bowl, whisk egg whites until stiff peaks form. Working in two batches, gently fold whites with a large flexible spatula into ricotta mixture until just combined.

2 Pour mixture into prepared dish and bake until puffed, golden brown, and firm to the touch, 30 to 32 minutes. Serve immediately.

Per serving: 220 calories, 14 g fat (7 g saturated fat), 245 mg cholesterol, 6 g carbohydrates, 17 g protein, 0 g fiber

VERSATILE VEGETARIAN:
LASAGNA

It's easy to omit the usual ground beef or sausage in a classic lasagna and to work vegetables into the mix, whether it's kale (see below), butternut squash (see page 184), or a host of others—mushrooms, eggplant, zucchini, and more.

LAYER NOODLES

ADD FILLING

FINISH WITH CHEESE

KALE LASAGNA SERVES 8

2 bunches kale (about 2 pounds total), tough stems removed

16 ounces (2 cups) part-skim ricotta cheese

1 large egg

¾ teaspoon coarse salt

6 cups Tomato Sauce (page 367)

16 no-boil whole-wheat lasagna noodles (10 ounces)

1 cup grated Parmigiano-Reggiano (about 2 ounces)

10 ounces fresh mozzarella, thinly sliced

Crushed red pepper flakes, for garnish

1. Preheat oven to 375°F. Wash kale; drain, leaving water clinging to leaves. Heat a large skillet over medium. Add kale; cover and cook until tender and bright green, 3 to 4 minutes. Transfer to a colander and let cool slightly; squeeze out excess moisture. Coarsely chop; you should have 4 cups.

2. Combine ricotta, egg, and salt in a medium bowl.

3. Spread 1 cup tomato sauce in a 9-by-13-inch baking dish. Layer 4 noodles over sauce. Spread one-third of the ricotta mixture and kale over noodles, and sprinkle with one-third of the Parmigiano-Reggiano.

Repeat layering (noodles, sauce, ricotta mixture, kale, and Parmigiano-Reggiano) two more times. Add final layer of noodles and spread with remaining sauce; arrange sliced mozzarella on top.

4. Cover dish with parchment, then foil. Bake until sauce is bubbling and noodles are tender, 45 to 50 minutes. Uncover and cook until cheese is lightly browned, about 10 minutes more. Let stand for 15 minutes before serving, garnished with red pepper flakes.

Per serving: 462 calories, 23.13 g fat (9.72 g saturated fat), 77.47 mg cholesterol, 40.13 g carbohydrates, 25.96 g protein, 7.72 g fiber

Roasted Butternut Squash Lasagna SERVES 8

- 2 large butternut squashes (about 4 pounds total), halved lengthwise and seeded
- 3 tablespoons extra-virgin olive oil

  Coarse salt and freshly ground pepper
- 2¼ cups finely grated Parmigiano-Reggiano (about 8 ounces), plus more if needed
- ¼ cup finely chopped fresh sage leaves, plus more if needed
- ¼ teaspoon freshly grated nutmeg, plus more if needed

  Béchamel Sauce (page 367)
- 16 no-boil whole-wheat lasagna noodles (10 ounces)

1. Preheat oven to 400°F. Drizzle squash halves with olive oil, and season with salt and pepper. Place cut sides down on a rimmed baking sheet and roast until tender, about 1 hour. Let cool. Scoop flesh from skins, and puree in a food processor until smooth.

2. Combine 3 cups squash puree, 1 cup cheese, the sage, 1 teaspoon salt, and the nutmeg in a medium bowl. Adjust seasoning as desired with more cheese, sage, salt, and nutmeg.

3. Reduce oven temperature to 375°F. Coat bottom and sides of a 9-by-13-inch baking dish with a thin layer of béchamel (about ½ cup). Arrange 4 noodles over sauce. Spread with ¾ cup squash filling, and top with 4 more noodles, then ¾ cup béchamel and 2 tablespoons cheese. Repeat layering (noodles, squash, noodles, béchamel, and cheese) one more time. Add final layer of noodles and spread with remaining béchamel.

4. Cover with parchment, then foil, and bake 20 minutes. Uncover, and sprinkle with remaining cheese. Bake until bubbling and top is browned, about 35 minutes more. Let cool slightly before serving.

Per serving: 665 calories, 29.11 g fat (14.52 g saturated fat), 65.82 mg cholesterol, 76.52 g carbohydrates, 26.32 g protein, 7.54 g fiber

substantial salads

Farro Salad with Oven-Roasted Grapes

This lovely whole-grain salad is flavored by two kinds of grapes that have been roasted in a low oven. **SERVES 12**

3 cups seedless red grapes (about 1 pound), halved

Coarse salt and freshly ground pepper

2 bunches Concord grapes

8 ounces farro (about 1½ cups)

2 tablespoons coarsely chopped fresh rosemary leaves

¼ cup extra-virgin olive oil

2 small red onions, sliced into ¼-inch-thick rounds

1 tablespoon sherry vinegar or red-wine vinegar

4 cups mixed tender young greens such as baby kale, baby Swiss chard, red mustard, and red mizuna

1 Preheat oven to 250°F. Spread red grapes on a rimmed baking sheet. Sprinkle with ¾ teaspoon salt. Place Concord grapes in middle of sheet. Bake until grapes have shrunk but are still juicy, about 1 hour 30 minutes. Let cool.

2 Meanwhile, combine farro, 1 tablespoon rosemary, and 1½ teaspoons salt in a saucepan; cover with water by 1 inch. Bring to a simmer; cook until tender, 25 minutes. Drain; transfer to a bowl.

3 Heat 1 tablespoon olive oil in a skillet over medium-high. Cook onions and remaining rosemary 2 minutes. Reduce heat to medium; cook until onions are golden brown, about 2 minutes more. Add 1 tablespoon oil. Flip onions, and season with salt. Cook, flipping, until onions are browned on both sides, 8 to 10 minutes. Remove from heat. Stir in vinegar and remaining oil. Toss mixture with farro. Season with salt and pepper. Stir in red grapes. Let stand 20 minutes.

4 To serve, stir in greens, arrange salad on a platter, and garnish with Concord grapes.

V Per serving: 188 calories, 5 g fat, (1 g saturated fat), 0 mg cholesterol, 34.61 g carbohydrates, 3.98 g protein, 2.73 g fiber

Fennel and Quinoa Salad with Parsley and Dill

For a study in contrasts, crisp, thinly shaved fennel is seasoned with parsley, dill, lemon juice, and olive oil, then served atop chewy, nutty-tasting quinoa. **SERVES 4**

- 1 fennel bulb (about 8 ounces), trimmed
- 1 cup quinoa, rinsed and drained
- 2 cups water
- 1 cup fresh flat-leaf parsley leaves
- 2 tablespoons chopped fresh dill
- ¼ cup fresh lemon juice (from 2 to 3 lemons)
- 1 tablespoon extra-virgin olive oil
  Coarse salt and freshly ground pepper

1 Prepare an ice-water bath. Cut fennel bulb in half lengthwise. Using a mandoline or adjustable-blade slicer, cut lengthwise as thin as possible. Place in ice bath.

2 Toast quinoa in a small saucepan over medium heat, stirring constantly, 5 minutes. Add the water and bring to a boil. Reduce to a simmer; cover, and cook 15 minutes. Remove from heat, and let stand, covered, 5 minutes. Transfer to a bowl; refrigerate, uncovered, until cool, about 1 hour.

3 Drain fennel, and pat dry with a paper towel. Place in large bowl. Add parsley, dill, lemon juice, and olive oil; season with salt and pepper, and toss to combine. Divide quinoa among 4 bowls. Top with fennel mixture and serve.

V G S Per serving: 219 calories, 6 g fat (1 g saturated fat), 0 mg cholesterol, 36 g carbohydrates, 7 g protein, 5 g fiber

Arugula, Potato, and Green Bean Salad with Walnut Dressing

Finely chopped toasted walnuts bulk up the yogurt dressing for this gorgeous salad. It's pretty enough to serve to company, either as the main course of a vegetarian meal or as a meatless offering at a summer potluck. **SERVES 8**

2 tablespoons white-wine vinegar

2 tablespoons plain low-fat yogurt

1 teaspoon Dijon mustard

⅓ cup walnuts, toasted (see page 363) and finely chopped

Coarse salt and freshly ground pepper

2 tablespoons walnut oil

1½ pounds fingerling potatoes, cut crosswise into ½-inch-thick rounds

6 ounces haricots verts or other green beans, trimmed

3 ounces baby arugula

1 Whisk together vinegar, yogurt, mustard, and the toasted nuts in a small bowl; season with salt and pepper. Add walnut oil in a slow, steady stream, whisking until emulsified.

2 Bring a medium saucepan of salted water to a boil. Add potatoes, and cook until tender, about 10 minutes. Using a slotted spoon, transfer potatoes to a colander to drain. Return pan of water to a boil.

3 Prepare an ice-water bath. Add green beans to boiling water and cook until tender and bright green, about 4 minutes. Using a slotted spoon, transfer to ice water to stop the cooking. Drain and cut into 2-inch pieces.

4 Arrange arugula, potatoes, and green beans on a platter. Season with salt and pepper. Drizzle with dressing, toss to coat, and serve.

G Per serving: 122 calories, 6 g fat (1 g saturated fat), 0 mg cholesterol, 17 g carbohydrates, 4 g protein, 3 g fiber

Fatoush with Crumbled Feta

This popular Middle Eastern salad combines whole-grain pita, kidney beans, and cucumber; in this version, feta is sprinkled over the top. The longer it sits, the more the toasted pita pieces soak up the delicious dressing. **SERVES 4**

1 whole-grain pita (6-inch size)

2 tablespoons extra-virgin olive oil, plus more for drizzling

Coarse salt and freshly ground pepper

1½ cups cooked red kidney beans (see page 365), drained and rinsed

½ English cucumber, chopped

1 shallot, diced

½ cup fresh flat-leaf parsley leaves

1 tablespoon fresh lemon juice

2 tablespoons crumbled feta

Toast pita over the flame of a gas burner (or char under the broiler). Drizzle with olive oil and season with salt. Tear into pieces and toss with kidney beans, cucumber, shallot, parsley, lemon juice, and olive oil in a large bowl. Top with crumbled feta, season with salt and pepper, and serve.

Per serving: 238 calories, 10.91 g fat (2.13 g saturated fat), 4.17 mg cholesterol, 27.84 g carbohydrates, 8.45 g protein, 6.26 g fiber

Roasted Eggplant Caprese Salad

Roasted eggplant slices are layered among the tomatoes and mozzarella in this update on Caprese salad. Fresh mozzarella has a creamier consistency than packaged varieties, and is the best type to use in salads such as this. **SERVES 6**

¼ cup plus 2 tablespoons olive oil

1 eggplant, cut crosswise into ¼-inch-thick rounds

Coarse salt and freshly ground pepper

1 pound fresh mozzarella, sliced into ¼-inch-thick rounds

1 pound tomatoes, sliced into ¼-inch-thick rounds

¼ cup loosely packed fresh basil leaves, torn

2 tablespoons balsamic vinegar (optional)

1 Preheat oven to 400°F. Brush each of 2 rimmed baking sheets with 1 tablespoon olive oil. Arrange eggplant slices in a single layer on sheets. Brush tops with 2 tablespoons oil, dividing evenly, and season with salt and pepper. Roast until eggplant is golden and tender, about 20 minutes. Let cool to room temperature.

2 Arrange eggplant, cheese, and tomatoes on a serving platter, slightly overlapping and alternating among components. Top with basil, drizzle with remaining 2 tablespoons oil and the balsamic vinegar, if desired, and serve.

G Per serving: 350 calories, 26.7 g fat (11.3 g saturated fat), 12.6 mg cholesterol, 10.6 g carbohydrates, 18.5 g protein, 4.3 g fiber

Bulgur and Chickpea Salad with Carrot-Pistachio Dressing

A raw carrot and pistachio pesto imparts even more Middle Eastern flavors to a salad of bulgur, chickpeas, mint, and dried fruit. The pesto would also work as a dressing for mixed fresh herbs and baby lettuces. **SERVES 4**

- ½ cup cracked bulgur wheat
- ¾ cup boiling water
- Coarse salt and freshly ground pepper
- 1½ cups cooked chickpeas (see page 365), drained and rinsed
- 1 scallion, trimmed and thinly sliced
- ¼ cup dried fruit, such as currants, golden raisins, or chopped apricots
- ½ cup fresh mint leaves, torn if large
- 2 carrots, peeled and chopped (1 cup)
- 1 small garlic clove, chopped
- ¼ cup shelled pistachios, toasted (see page 363)
- ¼ cup extra-virgin olive oil
- 1 lemon wedge

1. Place bulgur in a large heatproof bowl and add the boiling water. Season with a pinch of salt and cover with a plate until water is absorbed and bulgur is tender, about 30 minutes. Fluff with a fork. Stir in chickpeas, scallion, dried fruit, and mint.

2. Meanwhile, pulse carrots, garlic, and pistachios in a food processor until coarsely chopped. Drizzle in olive oil and process until combined. Season with salt and pepper.

3. Stir pesto into bulgur mixture. Squeeze lemon wedge over the salad and season with more salt and pepper, if desired, before serving.

Ⓥ Per serving: 397 calories, 19 g fat (2 g saturated fat), 0 mg cholesterol, 49 g carbohydrates, 10 g protein, 11 g fiber

New Greek Salad

All the familiar components—cucumbers, tomatoes, red onion, and slices of feta—of the diner classic remain in this updated version, along with fried kalamata olives and golden croutons made from olive bread. **SERVES 4**

1 cup olive oil, for frying

½ loaf olive bread, cut into ½-inch cubes (about 2 cups)

½ cup pitted kalamata olives

¼ cup plus 2 tablespoons extra-virgin olive oil

2 tablespoons red-wine vinegar

Coarse salt and freshly ground pepper

2 cups cherry tomatoes, quartered

1 cucumber, peeled and coarsely chopped

3 tablespoons chopped fresh dill

½ small red onion, thinly sliced

1 block feta (6 ounces), sliced ½ inch thick

1 Heat olive oil in a large high-sided skillet over high until it reaches 360°F on a deep-fry thermometer. Working in batches, fry bread and olives until golden, about 5 minutes. Transfer the croutons and olives to a paper-towel-lined plate using a slotted spoon.

2 Whisk together the extra-virgin olive oil and vinegar. Season with salt and pepper. Combine tomatoes, cucumber, dill, and onion in a large bowl. Add vinaigrette and toss to combine. Arrange feta on a platter. Top with tomato mixture, croutons, and olives, and serve.

Per serving: 704 calories, 49.88 g fat (12.31 g saturated fat), 37.85 mg cholesterol, 52.15 g carbohydrates, 15.06 g protein, 3.56 g fiber

Roasted-Tomato Tabbouleh

Basil is added to the standard parsley and mint combination in this version of the Middle-Eastern grain salad. Serve the tabbouleh with hummus and warm pitas, and, if desired, a platter of olives and store-bought stuffed grape leaves. **SERVES 4**

1 cup cracked bulgur wheat

1 cup boiling water

1 cup basil leaves, finely chopped, plus whole leaves for garnish

1 cup mint leaves, finely chopped, plus whole leaves for garnish

1 cup flat-leaf parsley leaves, coarsely chopped, plus whole leaves for garnish

4 plum tomatoes, cut into wedges

1 garlic clove, minced

2 tablespoons sherry vinegar

1 tablespoon extra-virgin olive oil

2 scallions, white and pale-green parts only, thinly sliced

Juice of 1 lemon

Coarse salt and freshly ground pepper

1. Preheat oven to 425°F. Place bulgur in a large heatproof bowl, add boiling water, and stir to combine. Cover tightly, and refrigerate until liquid has been absorbed, about 1 hour.

2. Combine chopped herbs in a small bowl. On a rimmed baking sheet, toss tomatoes with garlic, vinegar, 1 teaspoon olive oil, and 2 tablespoons chopped herbs. Roast until tomatoes begin to soften, about 12 minutes. Let cool.

3. Add roasted-tomato mixture, remaining chopped herbs, the scallions, lemon juice, and remaining 2 teaspoons oil to bulgur. Season with salt and pepper, and gently toss. Garnish with whole herb leaves and serve.

V Per serving: 184 calories, 4 g fat (1 g saturated fat), 0 mg cholesterol, 33 g carbohydrates, 6 g protein, 9 g fiber

Sprouted Summer Salad

Sprouted grains, which are thought to be easier to digest when uncooked, are a staple of raw-food diets. In this refreshing—and surprisingly filling—salad, sprouted quinoa is combined with sliced pineapple, cashews, and fresh mint. See note below for instructions on how to sprout your own quinoa. **SERVES 6**

¼ cup white-wine vinegar

¼ cup extra-virgin olive oil

Sea salt

1 small fresh hot chile, sliced into thin rings

½ red onion, thinly sliced

1 pineapple, peeled, cored, and sliced

¼ cup cashews

½ cup sprouted quinoa

¼ cup fresh mint leaves

1. In a small bowl, whisk vinegar and olive oil. Season with salt. Add chile and onion and toss. Let stand 10 minutes.

2. Arrange pineapple on a platter. Top with cashews, sprouted quinoa, and mint. Drizzle with chile-onion mixture and serve.

V G Per serving: 233 calories, 12 g fat (2 g saturated fat), 0 mg cholesterol, 30 g carbohydrates, 3 g protein, 3 g fiber

NOTE: To sprout quinoa, place ¼ cup quinoa in a Mason jar and cover top with cheesecloth. Secure with metal ring or rubber bands. Fill jar with water and let quinoa soak overnight. Drain. Rinse quinoa with water and drain twice a day for up to 2 days, until roots are about ½ inch long. (Quinoa should not dry out completely.) Once sprouted, rinse thoroughly and use immediately or transfer to an airtight container and refrigerate for up to 2 days. Makes ½ cup sprouted quinoa.

Eggplant Salad with Israeli Couscous and Basil

Pairing pasta with late-summer produce is an enticing way to usher in the comfort foods of autumn. Orzo can be used in place of the couscous in this recipe. **SERVES 4**

¾ cup Israeli (or pearl) couscous

1 cup water

Coarse salt and freshly ground pepper

3 tablespoons olive oil

1 pound Italian or graffiti eggplants, cut into ½-inch chunks

3 shallots, trimmed and quartered

2 teaspoons red-wine vinegar

⅓ cup lightly packed fresh basil leaves, torn

1 In a small saucepan, combine couscous, water, and ½ teaspoon salt. Bring to a boil, stir once, and reduce to a simmer. Cover and cook until couscous is tender, about 15 minutes.

2 Meanwhile, in a large skillet with a tight-fitting lid, heat olive oil over medium-high. Add eggplant and shallots and stir to coat; season with salt and pepper. Cover and cook, stirring frequently, until shallots are caramelized and eggplant is cooked through, 10 to 12 minutes.

3 In a serving bowl, combine eggplant mixture and couscous. Stir in vinegar and basil, season with salt and pepper, and serve.

V Per serving: 239 calories, 10.7 g fat (1.4 g saturated fat), 0 mg cholesterol, 32.5 g carbohydrates, 5.1 g protein, 4.1 g fiber

Roasted Fall Vegetables and Lentil Salad

It's hard to resist the caramelized sweetness of roasted squash and carrots; pairing these vegetables with warm dressed lentils rounds out a lovely main course. Don't be tempted to skip the celery leaves: although delicate, they pack a lot of flavor. **SERVES 4**

½ pound carrots, peeled and halved lengthwise

1 red onion, cut into 1-inch wedges

1 small acorn squash, halved, seeds removed, cut into ½-inch slices

4 ounces brussels sprouts, halved

¼ cup plus 1 tablespoon extra-virgin olive oil

Coarse salt and freshly ground pepper

½ cup dried French green lentils, picked over and rinsed

1 shallot, halved

1 tablespoon plus 1 teaspoon apple cider vinegar

1 teaspoon Dijon mustard

1 celery stalk, thinly sliced, leaves reserved

1 Preheat oven to 425°F. Combine carrots, onion, squash, and brussels sprouts on 2 rimmed baking sheets. Drizzle with 2 tablespoons olive oil, and season with salt and pepper. Roast in an even layer, turning once, until caramelized and tender, about 30 minutes.

2 Meanwhile, place lentils and shallot in a medium saucepan and cover with water by 2 inches. Bring to a boil, then simmer, covered, until lentils are tender, about 20 minutes. Drain; discard shallot. Season with salt and pepper.

3 In a medium bowl, combine vinegar and mustard. Pour in remaining 3 tablespoons oil in a slow, steady stream, whisking constantly. Add warm lentils and sliced celery and toss with vinaigrette. Season with salt and pepper. Spoon lentil salad onto 4 plates and top with roasted vegetables. Garnish with celery leaves and serve.

V G S Per serving: 333 calories, 18 g fat (3 g saturated fat), 0 mg cholesterol, 38 g carbohydrates, 9 g protein, 7 g fiber

Raw Kale Salad with Pomegranate and Toasted Walnuts

Sweeter varieties of kale, including the purple-veined Red Russian and the darker green Lacinato (or "dinosaur"), are tender enough to eat raw. In this salad, the leaves are rubbed with a mixture of olive oil, lime juice, and fresh ginger until thoroughly coated. You could do this several hours ahead, then toss with the remaining ingredients just before serving. **SERVES 4**

1 bunch kale, tough stems removed, torn into bite-size pieces

2 tablespoons olive oil

1 tablespoon fresh lime juice

½ teaspoon grated peeled fresh ginger

½ cup pomegranate seeds (from half a pomegranate; see note on page 40)

2 tablespoons chopped red onion

¼ cup chopped toasted walnuts (see page 363)

Coarse salt and freshly ground pepper

1 Place kale in a large salad bowl and add olive oil, lime juice, and ginger. Rub kale until well coated.

2 Add pomegranate seeds, onion, and walnuts and toss to combine. Season with salt and pepper and serve.

V G Per serving: 177 calories, 13 g fat (2 g saturated fat), 0 mg cholesterol, 14.85 g carbohydrates, 5 g protein, 3 g fiber

French Lentils with Caramelized Celery Root and Parsley

Once caramelized, celery root has a citrusy, licorice-like flavor that pairs well with lentils. Other root vegetables, including turnips, rutabagas, and parsnips, are also good options. **SERVES 4**

2 cups water

¾ cup dried French green lentils, picked over and rinsed

1 tablespoon plus 1 teaspoon extra-virgin olive oil

1 celery root (about 1 pound), washed well, peeled, and cut into ½-inch pieces

1 cup fresh flat-leaf parsley leaves

2 tablespoons fresh lemon juice

1 small shallot, minced

Coarse salt and freshly ground pepper

1 Bring the water and lentils to a boil in a medium saucepan. Reduce heat, and gently simmer, partially covered, until lentils are just tender, about 20 minutes. Drain lentils, and transfer to a medium bowl.

2 Meanwhile, heat 1 teaspoon olive oil in a medium nonstick high-sided skillet over medium. Cook celery root, stirring occasionally, until caramelized, 18 to 20 minutes.

3 Add celery root to bowl with lentils. Stir in parsley, lemon juice, shallot, and remaining tablespoon oil. Season with salt and pepper. Serve warm or at room temperature.

V G S Per serving: 209 calories, 5 g fat (1 g saturated fat), 0 mg cholesterol, 33 g carbohydrates, 9 g protein, 7 g fiber

Roasted Beet and Carrot Salad

Crisp endive leaves, tender roasted beets and carrots, tangy crumbled goat cheese, and buttery toasted pecans meld together with a citrus-tarragon vinaigrette. Frisée can be used in place of endive; you will need two heads for this recipe. **SERVES 4**

2 pounds red and golden beets, scrubbed, peeled, and thinly sliced

6 carrots, peeled and thinly sliced

3 tablespoons extra-virgin olive oil

Coarse salt and freshly ground pepper

3 tablespoons fresh orange juice

1½ teaspoons sherry vinegar

1½ teaspoons chopped fresh tarragon leaves

3 small Belgian endives, trimmed, halved lengthwise, and cut into 1-inch pieces

4 ounces fresh goat cheese, crumbled (about 1 cup)

⅓ cup chopped toasted pecans (see page 363)

1 Preheat oven to 450°F. On a rimmed baking sheet, toss beets and carrots with 1 tablespoon plus 1½ teaspoons olive oil; season with salt and pepper. Roast in a single layer until tender, 25 to 30 minutes, tossing halfway through. Let cool 5 minutes.

2 Meanwhile, in a small bowl, whisk together orange juice, vinegar, tarragon, and remaining 1 tablespoon plus 1½ teaspoons oil; season with salt and pepper.

3 In a large bowl, toss endives with half the dressing, then transfer to a serving platter. Toss beets and carrots with remaining dressing and add to platter. Top salad with goat cheese and pecans just before serving.

G Per serving: 378 calories, 23 g fat (6 g saturated fat), 13 mg cholesterol, 36 g carbohydrates, 12 g protein, 12 g fiber

Broccoli Rabe with Chickpeas and Ricotta

Broiling is one of the easiest ways to cook broccoli rabe: the stalks turn bright green and tender as the leaves crisp. Here, chickpeas are broiled alongside to make a warm salad or, for a heartier dish, a topping for whole-wheat pasta. **SERVES 4**

1 bunch broccoli rabe (about 12 ounces), rinsed and trimmed

1½ cups cooked chickpeas (see page 365), drained and rinsed

2 garlic cloves, sliced

3 tablespoons extra-virgin olive oil, plus more for drizzling

Coarse salt

1 cup part-skim ricotta cheese (8 ounces)

2 tablespoons fresh lemon juice

Crushed red pepper flakes

1 Heat broiler, with rack 4 inches from the heat source. On 2 rimmed baking sheets, toss broccoli rabe, chickpeas, and garlic with olive oil; season with salt. Spread in a single layer and broil 2 minutes, then flip broccoli rabe and continue to broil until leaves are crisp and stems are tender, about 2 minutes more. (Broil one tray at a time if your oven can't accommodate both.)

2 To serve, top with ricotta, lemon juice, and a drizzle of oil; sprinkle with red pepper flakes.

G Per serving: 334 calories, 16 g fat (5 g saturated fat), 25 mg cholesterol, 32 g carbohydrates, 15 g protein, 8 g fiber

Steamed Broccoli and Squash with Tahini Sauce

To make a satisfying meal out of virtuous steamed vegetables, serve them atop salad greens drizzled with a rich tahini sauce. These veggies are steamed just until their color brightens and they become tender yet still retain a bit of bite. Use any leftover sauce to dress other salads or to top falafel or vegetable burgers. **SERVES 4**

½ head broccoli (about ½ pound), cut into florets

1 delicata squash (about 1 pound), sliced and seeded

1 cup mixed tender greens, such as arugula, baby spinach, and mizuna

1 cup thinly sliced red cabbage

2 tablespoons diced red onion

Coarse salt and freshly ground pepper

Tahini Sauce (page 369)

1 tablespoon toasted sesame seeds (see page 363)

1. Place a steamer basket or colander in a medium saucepan filled with 2 inches of water. Bring water to a boil, then reduce to a simmer. Place broccoli in basket, cover, and steam until bright green and just tender, about 5 minutes. Transfer to a plate. Place squash in basket and cook until bright yellow and tender, about 10 minutes.

2. In a bowl, toss together greens, cabbage, and red onion. Top with steamed vegetables. Season with salt and pepper. Drizzle with ¼ cup tahini sauce, sprinkle with toasted sesame seeds, and serve.

V G S Per serving: 109 calories, 6 g fat (1 g saturated fat), 0 mg cholesterol, 12.58 g carbohydrate, 4 g protein, 4 g fiber

Avocado, Beet, and Orange Salad

A crunchy component or two helps create a more interesting salad. Here, the crunch is provided by toasted sunflower seeds and croutons. To make the crispiest croutons, tear the bread rather than slicing it: the rough edges will soak up more olive oil. **SERVES 4**

1	small bunch beets (about 1 pound), trimmed
2	slices rustic bread, torn into 1-inch pieces (2 cups)
¼	cup extra-virgin olive oil
	Coarse salt and freshly ground pepper
2	teaspoons balsamic vinegar
2	tablespoons fresh orange juice
2	firm, ripe avocados, halved, pitted, peeled, and sliced
2	navel oranges, peel and pith removed, segmented
2	cups spinach (trimmed, washed well, and drained)
1	tablespoon toasted salted sunflower seeds (see page 363)

1 Preheat oven to 425°F. Wrap beets tightly in parchment, then foil. Place on a rimmed baking sheet, and roast until tender, about 1 hour. Let cool slightly, then rub off skins with paper towels. Slice beets into wedges.

2 Meanwhile, toss bread pieces with 2 tablespoons olive oil, season with salt and pepper, and toast on a rimmed baking sheet until golden, about 6 minutes.

3 Whisk together vinegar, orange juice, and remaining 2 tablespoons oil in a small bowl; season with salt and pepper. Combine beets, avocados, oranges, spinach, and croutons in a large bowl or on a serving platter. Drizzle vinaigrette over salad and season with salt and pepper. Top with sunflower seeds, and serve.

V Per serving: 236 calories, 19 g fat (3 g saturated fat), 0 mg cholesterol, 15 g carbohydrates, 3 g protein, 4 g fiber

Shaved Parsnip Salad

Crunchy, mildly sweet parsnips are delicious when shaved very thin and tossed with lettuce and dates, as in this quick salad. The flavors make it ideal for the Thanksgiving table, or as part of any other seasonal celebration. **SERVES 8**

2 tablespoons sherry vinegar

3 tablespoons extra-virgin olive oil

Coarse salt and freshly ground pepper

2 hearts of romaine, cut into bite-size pieces

3 parsnips (about 8 ounces), peeled and shaved very thin (on a mandoline or other adjustable-blade slicer, or with a vegetable peeler)

4 Medjool or 6 regular dates, pitted and cut into ½-inch pieces

1 Whisk together vinegar and olive oil in a small bowl; season with salt and pepper.

2 In a large bowl, toss lettuce, parsnips, and dates. Drizzle with dressing. Season with salt and pepper, and serve.

V G S Per serving: 105 calories, 5 g fat (1 g saturated fat), 0 mg cholesterol, 15 g carbohydrates, 1 g protein, 3 g fiber

Warm Edamame Salad

Using frozen edamame is a convenient way to add protein to Asian soups and salads such as this one. It gets lots of interesting textures from water chestnuts, mushrooms, and snap peas, and spicy flavors by way of fresh ginger and hot chile sauce. Serve the salad with brown rice or soba noodles. **SERVES 4**

2 tablespoons canola oil

4 cups cremini mushrooms (12 ounces), sliced

16 ounces frozen shelled edamame, thawed

1 cup sugar snap peas (4 ounces), sliced in half

1 teaspoon minced peeled fresh ginger

½ cup roasted red bell peppers (see page 364), cut into ½-inch strips

1 can (8 ounces) sliced water chestnuts, drained

½ teaspoon Asian hot chile sauce, preferably Sriracha

Coarse salt and freshly ground pepper

1 tablespoon toasted sesame seeds (see page 363)

2 teaspoons rice vinegar (unseasoned)

1 Heat 1 tablespoon oil in a large pan over medium-high. Cook the mushrooms, stirring, until tender, 6 to 8 minutes. Transfer to a bowl.

2 Add remaining tablespoon oil to pan. Cook the edamame, snap peas, and ginger, stirring occasionally, until peas are tender and edamame is bright green, 3 to 5 minutes.

3 Add the red pepper, water chestnuts, chile sauce, and mushrooms; cook, stirring, until heated through, about 2 minutes. Season with salt and pepper. Remove from heat; stir in toasted sesame seeds and the vinegar. Serve warm.

V G Per serving: 347 calories, 13 g fat (1 g saturated fat), 0 mg cholesterol, 38 g carbohydrates, 17 g protein, 10 g fiber

Kale, Apple, and Beet Salad

Join the raw-food movement: here, thin slices of beet (achieved with a mandoline or other adjustable-blade slicer) and apple wedges complement the bitterness of coarsely chopped kale. The secret ingredient in the thick, creamy dressing that brings everything into balance is pureed avocado. **SERVES 4**

1 firm, ripe avocado, halved, pitted, and peeled

2 tablespoons white-wine vinegar

2 teaspoons Dijon mustard

3 tablespoons walnut oil or extra-virgin olive oil

Coarse salt and freshly ground pepper

½ bunch kale (about 8 ounces), stemmed and coarsely chopped

1 small red beet, peeled and thinly sliced

1 sweet, crisp apple, cored and cut into thin wedges

½ cup walnuts, chopped

1 Combine avocado, vinegar, mustard, and oil in a food processor. Pulse until smooth (it will be thick). Season dressing with salt and pepper.

2 Combine kale, beet, apple, and walnuts in a large bowl. Toss with avocado dressing. Season with salt and pepper, and serve immediately.

V G Per serving: 325 calories, 27 g fat (3 g saturated fat), 0 mg cholesterol, 19.19 g carbohydrates, 5.52 g protein, 6.88 g fiber

Roasted Squash, Apple, and Cipollini Onion Salad

This colorful salad is a cinch to make—the oven does most of the work—and is loaded with nutritious vegetables and fruit, notably watercress and roasted squash and apples. **SERVES 4**

½ butternut squash or sugar pumpkin, peeled, seeded, and cut into ½-inch pieces (3 cups)

1½ teaspoons olive oil, plus more for drizzling

Coarse salt and freshly ground pepper

2 Golden Delicious apples, peeled and cut into ½-inch-thick wedges

8 cipollini onions, peeled, trimmed, and sliced crosswise into ¼-inch-thick rings

4 cups watercress, tough ends trimmed

1½ teaspoons sherry vinegar

¼ cup chopped toasted walnuts (see page 363)

1 Preheat oven to 400°F. Drizzle squash with olive oil and season with salt and pepper on a rimmed baking sheet; toss to combine and spread in a single layer. Roast, tossing halfway through, until squash is tender and browned, 40 to 45 minutes.

2 Meanwhile, drizzle apples and onions with oil and season with salt and pepper on another rimmed baking sheet; toss and spread in a single layer. Roast, tossing halfway through, until apples are tender and lightly browned and onions are just starting to crisp, 25 to 30 minutes.

3 Toss watercress with the oil and vinegar in a bowl; season with salt and pepper. Transfer salad to a serving platter, and top with apple-onion mixture, squash, and walnuts. Serve immediately.

V G Per serving: 222 calories, 8 g fat (1 g saturated fat), 0 mg cholesterol, 37 g carbohydrates, 5 g protein, 7 g fiber

Tofu with Tomatoes, Basil, and Mint

Soft tofu stands in for mozzarella in a vegan version of Caprese salad. Soy sauce, toasted sesame seeds, and fresh mint contribute more Asian flavors to the dish. **SERVES 6**

1 tablespoon plus 1 teaspoon sherry vinegar

2 teaspoons low-sodium soy sauce

¼ cup extra-virgin olive oil

14 ounces (1 package) soft tofu, drained

2 pounds mixed ripe tomatoes, cut into ½-inch-thick slices (halve cherry tomatoes)

Coarse salt and freshly ground pepper

1 tablespoon fresh basil leaves, thinly sliced, plus whole leaves for garnish

1 tablespoon fresh mint leaves, thinly sliced, plus whole leaves for garnish

2 teaspoons sesame seeds, toasted (see page 363)

1 Whisk together vinegar, soy sauce, and olive oil in a small bowl. Halve tofu crosswise, then cut horizontally into ¼-inch-thick squares.

2 Arrange tofu and tomatoes on a platter and season with salt and pepper. Drizzle with dressing and top with sliced herbs and sesame seeds. Garnish with basil and mint leaves and serve.

V Per serving: 164 calories, 12 g fat (2 g saturated fat), 0 mg cholesterol, 10 g carbohydrates, 5 g protein, 2 g fiber

VERSATILE VEGETARIAN:
GRAIN SALAD

Consider this recipe a blueprint for making delicious main-course salads based on whole grains—quinoa, brown rice, barley, and farro, to name just a few. Almost any vegetables, herbs, spices, and other components can be mixed in. The variations here keep beautifully in the refrigerator for a few days.

COOK THE GRAINS

PREPARE THE ADD-INS

TOSS THE SALAD

QUINOA SALAD WITH TOASTED ALMONDS SERVES 2

½ cup quinoa, rinsed and drained

1 tablespoon plus 1 teaspoon olive oil

1 yellow bell pepper, ribs and seeds removed, cut into ½-inch pieces

2 garlic cloves, minced

2 scallions, thinly sliced

⅛ teaspoon crushed red pepper flakes

1 teaspoon chopped fresh thyme leaves, plus more for garnish (optional)

1 zucchini, halved lengthwise and sliced

1 large celery stalk, diced

¼ cup slivered almonds, toasted (see page 363)

¼ teaspoon coarse salt

1 lime, halved

1. Combine quinoa and 1 cup water in a medium saucepan. Bring to a boil, then reduce to a simmer. Cover, and cook until quinoa is tender, 12 to 15 minutes. Remove from heat.

2. Meanwhile, heat 2 teaspoons olive oil in a medium saucepan over medium. Add bell pepper, garlic, scallions, and red pepper flakes; cook, stirring frequently, until the bell pepper has softened, about 5 minutes. Add thyme and zucchini; cook until tender, about 5 minutes.

3. Combine quinoa and zucchini mixture in a large bowl. Stir in celery, almonds, and remaining 2 teaspoons oil; season with

salt, and fluff with a fork. Cool completely before refrigerating, covered. Squeeze lime halves over salad and garnish with thyme, if desired, just before serving.

V G Per serving: 368 calories, 19 g fat (2.09 g saturated fat), 0 mg cholesterol, 44 g carbohydrates, 11 g protein, 7 g fiber

Wheat Berry Salad with Artichoke Hearts SERVES 6

- 1 shallot, minced
- Grated zest and juice of 1 lemon
- Coarse salt and freshly ground pepper
- 3 tablespoons olive oil
- ¼ cup pine nuts
- 3½ cups cooked wheat berries (see page 371)
- 1 can (14 ounces) artichoke hearts, drained and quartered
- ½ cup flat-leaf parsley leaves, chopped
- Shaved Parmigiano-Reggiano, for garnish

1. In a small bowl, combine shallot and lemon juice; season with salt. Let stand 15 minutes. Meanwhile, heat olive oil in a small pan over medium. Add pine nuts and cook, stirring, until lightly golden, about 2 minutes. Remove from heat and add lemon zest to pan.

2. In a large bowl, combine wheat berries, pine-nut mixture, artichoke hearts, and parsley. Stir in shallot mixture and season with salt and pepper. Cover and refrigerate until ready to serve; garnish with shaved parmesan just before serving.

Per serving: 375 calories, 18.12 g fat (2.89 g saturated fat), 8.32 mg cholesterol, 14.21 g carbohydrates, 13.88 g protein, 8.06 g fiber

Farro, Chickpea, and Feta Salad SERVES 4

- 2½ cups cooked farro (see page 371)
- 1 tablespoon plus 1½ teaspoons fresh lemon juice
- 1½ cups cooked chickpeas (see page 365), drained and rinsed
- 2 teaspoons finely grated lemon zest
- 3 tablespoons extra-virgin olive oil
- ¾ cup crumbled feta cheese (3 ounces)
- ½ cup grape or cherry tomatoes, halved
- ½ cup fresh mint leaves
- ¼ small red onion, finely chopped (optional)
- Coarse salt

Toss farro with lemon juice while still warm. Combine with chickpeas in a large bowl. Add lemon zest and olive oil, toss to combine, and let cool to room temperature. Stir in feta, tomatoes, mint, and onion, if using; season with salt. Cover and refrigerate until ready to serve.

Per serving: 457 calories, 15.85 g fat (4.67 saturated fat), 18.92 mg cholesterol, 61.4 g carbohydrates, 17.41 g protein, 8.15 g fiber

Brown Rice, Edamame, and Cilantro Salad SERVES 4

- 3 cups cooked brown rice (see page 371)
- 2 tablespoons rice vinegar (unseasoned)
- 1 cup thawed frozen shelled edamame
- 3 tablespoons low-sodium soy sauce
- 3 tablespoons water
- ¾ teaspoon toasted-sesame oil
- 2 cups shredded bok choy or Napa cabbage
- ½ cup fresh cilantro
- 1 tablespoons toasted sesame seeds (see page 363), for garnish
- Lime wedges, for serving

Toss rice with vinegar while still warm. Steam edamame in a pan of simmering water until bright green and tender, about 2 minutes; drain. Whisk together soy sauce, the water, and toasted-sesame oil in a small bowl. Combine rice, bok choy or cabbage, cilantro, and edamame in a large bowl; stir in dressing. Cover and refrigerate until ready to serve. Garnish with sesame seeds and serve with lime wedges.

V Per serving: 248 calories, 5.22 g fat (0.4 g saturated fat), 0 mg cholesterol, 39.35 g carbohydrates, 10.62 g protein, 5.39 g fiber

**WHEAT BERRY SALAD WITH
ARTICHOKE HEARTS**

**FARRO, CHICKPEA,
AND FETA SALAD**

**BROWN RICE, EDAMAME,
AND CILANTRO SALAD**

sandwiches, burgers, and pizzas

Zucchini Patties in Pita Bread

These patties make good use of late-summer zucchini. They are quick to make, can be formed up to a day ahead, and take mere minutes to cook. Set them on a platter with pita, yogurt, lettuce, and mint alongside for an assemble-it-yourself dinner. Round out the meal with the orzo salad on page 282 (another great make-ahead dish). **SERVES 8**

1½ cups cooked chickpeas (see page 365), drained and rinsed

1 cup plain fresh bread crumbs

1 medium zucchini, grated

1 small red onion, grated

1 large egg, lightly whisked

1 teaspoon coarse salt

¼ cup olive oil

4 whole-wheat pitas (6 inch), toasted

1 cup plain Greek-style yogurt (2 percent)

8 leaves tender lettuce

1 cup fresh mint leaves

1 Mash chickpeas in a bowl until smooth. Stir in bread crumbs, zucchini, onion, egg, and salt. Form into eight ½-inch-thick patties. (Patties can be wrapped well in plastic and refrigerated overnight.)

2 Heat olive oil in a large skillet over medium-high. Sauté patties until golden and crisp, 2 to 3 minutes per side.

3 To serve, halve pitas and stuff with patties, yogurt, lettuce, and mint.

Per serving: 304 calories, 10 g fat (2 g saturated fat), 28 mg cholesterol, 45 g carbohydrates, 12 g protein, 9 g fiber

Chipotle Avocado Sandwiches

Mashed beans make a quick, protein-rich sandwich spread; chipotle chile is added to this one for rich, smoky flavor and fiery spice. Chipotles come packed in adobo sauce, a blend of herbs, spices, vinegar, and ground chiles that can also be used on its own (try stirring it into sauces, stews, or salad dressings for extra kick). **SERVES 4**

1½ cups cooked red kidney beans (see page 365), drained and rinsed

1 chipotle in adobo, finely chopped, plus 1 tablespoon sauce

Coarse salt and freshly ground pepper

8 slices whole-grain bread, toasted

1 firm, ripe avocado, halved, pitted, peeled, and sliced

4 radishes, trimmed and sliced

4 leaves escarole

1 cup bean sprouts (or other sprouts)

Mash beans, chipotle, and sauce until combined. Season with salt and pepper. Spread bean mixture on 4 slices of bread. Top with avocado, radishes, escarole, and sprouts. Sandwich with remaining bread and serve.

V Per serving: 325 calories, 9 g fat (2 g saturated fat), 0 mg cholesterol, 47 g carbohydrates, 13.38 g protein, 12.52 g fiber

Brussels Sprout and Lemon Skillet Pizza

A cast-iron skillet produces pizza with a delicious, golden brown crust; it's started on the stove to get the bottom nice and crisp before it bakes in the oven. In this recipe, brussels sprout leaves on top turn delightfully crunchy as they bake, while paper-thin lemon slices become tender and caramelized. You can also try one of the toppings on page 267. **SERVES 4**

1 tablespoon plus 1 teaspoon olive oil

¾ pound store-bought or homemade pizza dough (see page 267)

3 ounces fresh mozzarella, thinly sliced

1½ ounces finely grated Pecorino Romano (about ⅔ cup)

3 cups packed brussels sprout leaves (from about ½ pound)

Coarse salt and freshly ground pepper

5 paper-thin lemon slices (use an adjustable-blade slicer; remove seeds), cut into half-moons (from ½ lemon)

1 Preheat oven to 500°F. Brush a 12-inch cast-iron skillet with 1 teaspoon olive oil. Press dough flat in skillet, spreading to edge (if it retracts, let rest 5 minutes before continuing). Brush a 1-inch border around edge with 1 teaspoon oil.

2 Scatter mozzarella and half the Pecorino evenly over dough, leaving a ½-inch border around edge.

3 Toss brussels sprout leaves with remaining Pecorino, remaining 2 teaspoons oil, ¼ teaspoon salt, and ¼ teaspoon pepper. Scatter sprout mixture over dough, and top with lemon slices.

4 Cook over medium-high heat until bottom is golden brown, 4 to 5 minutes. Transfer to oven; bake until edges of sprouts darken, crust is golden and cooked through, about 10 minutes. Season with pepper and serve.

Per serving: 326 calories, 11.2 g fat (2.5 g saturated fat), 12.9 mg cholesterol, 43.12 g carbohydrates, 18.76 g protein, 4.12 g fiber

Portobello and Zucchini Tacos

Roasted vegetables make fine fillings for meat-free tacos; besides the ones used here, try corn, bell peppers, other types of mushrooms, and any variety of squash or potato. Rajas is another classic option: Roast four poblano chiles (see page 364), cut into half-inch-wide strips, and season with salt; serve with pickled red onion (see page 361) and shredded cheese. **SERVES 4**

5 portobello mushrooms, stemmed and sliced ½ inch thick

2 teaspoons dried oregano

2 tablespoons olive oil

¼ cup water

Coarse salt and freshly ground pepper

4 zucchini, cut into 2-by-½-inch sticks

1 red onion, halved and sliced ¼ inch thick

8 corn tortillas (4½-inch size)

6 ounces Monterey Jack, shredded (1½ cups)

1 cup cherry tomatoes, halved or quartered

1 Preheat oven to 425°F. On a rimmed baking sheet, toss mushrooms with 1 teaspoon oregano, 1 tablespoon olive oil, and the water; season with salt and pepper. On another baking sheet, toss zucchini and onion with remaining teaspoon oregano and tablespoon olive oil; season with salt and pepper.

2 Roast, tossing occasionally, until vegetables are browned and fork-tender, 25 to 30 minutes (zucchini may cook faster than mushrooms).

3 Using tongs, hold each tortilla directly over a gas flame, turning, until heated through, about 5 seconds. (Alternatively, wrap tortillas in parchment, then foil, and warm in a 350°F oven.)

4 To serve, fill each tortilla with mushrooms, vegetable mixture, shredded cheese, and tomatoes.

Ⓖ Per serving: 397 calories, 22 g fat (9.45 g saturated fat), 37.85 mg cholesterol, 35.6 g carbohydrates, 18.8 g protein, 5.2 g fiber

Chickpea–Brown Rice Burgers

Swap out the usual buns for lettuce-leaf wrappers, and meatless burgers are instantly more interesting—and lighter. These patties are made from chickpeas and brown rice. Other herbs, such as cilantro, basil, or mint, can be used in place of the parsley. **SERVES 4**

2 cups cooked chickpeas (see page 365), drained and rinsed

1 cup cooked brown rice (see page 371)

1 shallot, minced

1 garlic clove, minced

2 tablespoons chopped fresh flat-leaf parsley leaves

Coarse salt and freshly ground pepper

1 large egg

2 tablespoons olive oil

Whole-grain mustard, sliced red onion, and sliced roasted red peppers, for serving

Tender lettuce leaves, such as Boston or Bibb, for wrapping

1 Mash chickpeas and brown rice with a fork until a thick paste forms. Stir in shallot, garlic, and parsley. Season with salt and pepper. Whisk egg and stir into bean mixture. Form into four ½-inch-thick patties.

2 Heat olive oil in a large skillet over medium-high. Add patties and cook until golden brown, about 4 minutes per side.

3 To serve, spread each burger with mustard, top with red onion and roasted pepper, and wrap in lettuce leaves.

G Per serving: 250 calories, 5 g fat (1 g saturated fat), 52.88 mg cholesterol, 36.18 g carbohydrates, 9 g protein, 6 g fiber

Mushroom, Spinach, and Scallion Tart

Vibrant spinach leaves intermingle with roasted mushrooms in a light-as-air (and easy to assemble) phyllo shell. The custardlike filling comes together quickly in a blender. **SERVES 8**

1 pound mixed mushrooms such as button and shiitake, stemmed and sliced ½ inch thick

2 tablespoons olive oil, plus more for brushing

Coarse salt

12 scallions, trimmed and cut into 2-inch pieces

3½ cups spinach (about 4 ounces), stemmed, washed, and shaken dry

10 sheets frozen phyllo dough (14 by 9 inches each), thawed

6 ounces fresh goat cheese (about ⅔ cup)

3 large eggs

⅓ cup low-fat milk

3 tablespoons chopped mixed fresh herbs, such as dill and cilantro

1. Preheat oven to 425°F. On a rimmed baking sheet, toss mushrooms with 2 tablespoons olive oil and season with salt. Spread in a single layer and roast 10 minutes. Toss in the scallions and roast 15 minutes more. Push mushrooms and scallions to one side and place spinach on empty side; roast until wilted, about 3 minutes. Let cool briefly; squeeze spinach dry.

2. Lightly brush an 11-by-7-inch rectangular tart pan with a removable bottom (or a 10-inch round pan) with oil. Working with one piece of phyllo at a time and keeping the rest covered with plastic wrap, brush

a sheet of the pastry very lightly with oil. Fit into tart pan, leaving a 1-inch overhang. Brush a second sheet with oil and fit into pan. Repeat with remaining sheets. Fold edges at top to make a border.

3 Crumple a double layer of foil into a rectangle the size of the bottom of the tart and fit into crust to weigh down center. Place on a baking sheet and bake until edges are golden and begin to set, about 7 minutes. Remove foil and bake until golden all over, about 3 minutes more. (Tent edges with foil if browning too quickly.) Remove tart pan from oven.

4 Reduce oven to 375°F. In a blender, puree the goat cheese, eggs, and milk until smooth; season with salt. Add herbs and pulse to combine. Spread vegetables over crust and pour custard over top.

5 Return tart pan to oven and bake until custard is set, 20 to 23 minutes. Remove tart pan from oven and let cool 10 minutes on a wire rack. Remove sides of pan and let tart cool at least 10 minutes more. If not serving right away, slide tart off bottom of pan and directly onto rack. Serve warm or at room temperature.

Per serving: 268 calories, 16.54 g fat (5.34 g saturated fat), 89.91 mg cholesterol, 19.9 g carbohydrates, 10.76 g protein, 2.44 g fiber

Bean-and-Vegetable Sliders

These mini veggie burgers take their cue from the flavors of Vietnamese *banh mi* sandwiches, with carrot, broccoli, ginger, garlic, and cilantro added to the patties and chile-spiked mayonnaise and mango used as toppings. **SERVES 4**

1 tablespoon olive oil

½ onion, coarsely chopped

1 garlic clove, chopped

½ fresh chile, chopped

Coarse salt

2 cups cooked kidney beans (see page 365), drained and rinsed

1 cup cooked basmati rice (see page 371)

½ cup shredded carrot

½ cup finely chopped broccoli florets

2 tablespoons grated peeled fresh ginger

2 tablespoons finely chopped fresh cilantro

1 tablespoon canola oil

12 small whole-wheat rolls, split

Chile Mayonnaise (page 369)

Assorted garnishes, such as lettuce, cilantro, sliced mango, and sliced onion

1. Heat olive oil in a pot over medium. Add onion, garlic, and chile, and season with salt. Cook until onion is soft, stirring occasionally, about 5 minutes.

2. Pulse beans in a food processor to form a coarse mash. Pulse in rice. Stir bean mixture in a bowl with carrot, broccoli, ginger, cilantro, and onion mixture.

3. Form into twelve ½-inch-thick patties. Heat canola oil in a large skillet over medium-high. Cook patties in batches until golden and crisp, about 3 minutes per side. Place patties on rolls, top with chile mayonnaise and assorted garnishes as desired, and serve.

Per serving: 233 calories, 9.12 g fat (1.3 g saturated fat), 2.82 mg cholesterol, 33.55 g carbohydrates, 6.41 g protein, 4.97 g fiber

Broccoli Rabe Pizza with Hazelnut Dough

It's not just the toppings that make a pizza great—you can switch up the dough, too, by adding ground hazelnuts or other nuts such as pecans or walnuts. **SERVES 2**

- 1 small bunch broccoli rabe, trimmed and cut into 3-inch pieces

    Coarse salt

- 2 tablespoons extra-virgin olive oil, plus more for drizzling
- ½ red onion, very thinly sliced
- 1 or 2 pinches of crushed red pepper flakes
- ¼ cup fine yellow cornmeal
- 1 ball Hazelnut Pizza Dough (page 370)
- ¼ cup shaved Pecorino Romano

1. Preheat oven to 500°F. Blanch broccoli rabe in a pot of boiling salted water until tender, about 1 minute. Drain in a colander. Rinse under cold running water, then drain again. Toss broccoli rabe with olive oil, onion, and red pepper flakes; season with salt.

2. Spread cornmeal on a baking sheet. Stretch dough into a 9½-inch round; transfer to baking sheet. Drizzle dough with oil, and arrange broccoli rabe on top, leaving a ½-inch border. Bake until crust is golden brown and cooked through, about 20 minutes. Drizzle with more oil, top with cheese, and serve.

Per serving: 763 calories, 43.03 g fat (6.7 g saturated fat), 7.2 mg cholesterol, 74.91 g carbohydrates, 22.62 g protein, 3.95 g fiber

Butternut Squash Pizza with Hazelnut Dough

Thinly sliced squash is an unexpected and thoroughly modern pizza topper. Hazelnuts echo the flavor of the crust. **SERVES 2**

- 1 cup very thinly sliced peeled and seeded butternut squash

    Extra-virgin olive oil, for drizzling

    Coarse salt

- ¼ cup fine yellow cornmeal
- 1 ball Hazelnut Pizza Dough (page 370)
- 6 to 10 small fresh sage leaves (torn if large)
- 1 to 2 garlic cloves, thinly sliced

    Toasted, skinned (see page 363), and coarsely chopped hazelnuts, for garnish

1. Preheat oven to 500°F. Drizzle squash with oil in a bowl and season with salt.

2. Spread cornmeal on a baking sheet. Stretch dough into a 9½-inch round; transfer to baking sheet. Drizzle dough with oil, and arrange squash on top, leaving a ½-inch border. Bake 10 minutes. In same bowl, toss sage with garlic, and drizzle with oil to coat. Sprinkle sage mixture over pizza and continue to bake until crust is golden brown, 10 minutes more. Garnish with hazelnuts, drizzle with more oil, and serve.

V Per serving: 574 calories, 28.59 g fat (3.16 g saturated fat), 0 mg cholesterol, 70.10 g carbohydrates, 11.91 g protein, 5.01 g fiber

Crisp Tofu Sandwiches with Peanut-Ginger Sauce

An Asian-style sauce made from peanut butter, sesame oil, honey, and fresh ginger sets these make-ahead sandwiches apart from the rest. The sauce can also be used to make cold noodle salads or as a dip with crisp vegetables. **MAKES 2**

1 onion, cut into ½-inch-thick rounds

1 red bell pepper, ribs and seeds removed, quartered lengthwise

2 teaspoons olive oil

2 tablespoons natural peanut butter

½ teaspoon honey

½ teaspoon toasted-sesame oil

¾ teaspoon grated peeled fresh ginger

1 8-inch whole-grain baguette, split

½ recipe Marinated Tofu (page 365), cut into ½-inch-thick slices

Radish sprouts, for garnish (optional)

1. Heat broiler with rack 4 inches from heat source. Place onion and bell peppers, skin side up, on a broiler pan. Drizzle with olive oil. Broil, flipping onion halfway through, until peppers are blistered and onion is lightly browned, 12 to 15 minutes. When cool enough to handle, peel skin off peppers. Cut peppers into thick strips.

2. In a small bowl, combine peanut butter, honey, ¼ teaspoon sesame oil, and the ginger. Toss reserved vegetables with remaining ¼ teaspoon sesame oil.

3. Spread peanut-butter mixture on bottom half of bread. Top with tofu and vegetables, then sandwich with top bread half. Cut in half and garnish with radish sprouts, if desired.

V Per serving: 483 calories, 28.15 g fat (3.55 g saturated fat), 0 mg cholesterol, 43.26 g carbohydrates, 19.49 g protein, 7.35 g fiber

Cauliflower, Red Onion, and Chestnut Tart

With its combination of cauliflower, blue cheese, chestnuts, and pearl onions, this tart is perfect as a vegetarian main course at a holiday dinner, where it could easily double as a side dish for meat eaters. Chestnuts that have been peeled and packed in jars or bottles can be found at most supermarkets. **SERVES 8**

FOR THE CRUST

1 rectangle Hazelnut Pastry Dough (page 370)

All-purpose flour, for dusting

FOR THE FILLING

4 ounces red pearl onions

Coarse salt

1 small head cauliflower, trimmed and separated into florets

2 teaspoons olive oil

FOR THE BÉCHAMEL

2 tablespoons unsalted butter

2 tablespoons all-purpose flour

1 cup whole milk

½ cup crumbled blue cheese (2 ounces)

1 teaspoon chopped fresh thyme leaves

Coarse salt

⅓ cup coarsely chopped peeled chestnuts

1 Make the crust: Roll out pastry dough to a 6-by-16-inch rectangle on a lightly floured surface. Fit dough into a 4-by-13-inch fluted tart pan with a removable bottom. Trim edges flush with top. Prick bottom of tart all over with a fork. Refrigerate until firm, about 1 hour.

2 Preheat oven to 375°F. Line crust with parchment, leaving an overhang on all sides. Fill with pie weights or dried beans. Bake until crust is set and edges are just starting to turn golden brown, about 25 minutes. Remove pie weights and parchment. Bake until bottom of tart shell is pale gold, about 10 minutes more. Let cool completely on a wire rack. Reduce oven temperature to 350°F.

3 Meanwhile, make the filling: Prepare an ice-water bath. Blanch onions in a pot of boiling salted water 2 minutes. Transfer to the ice bath; drain. Squeeze onions from skins and cut each in half. Meanwhile, steam cauliflower in a steamer basket (or colander) set over a pan of simmering water, covered, until almost tender, about 3 minutes. Season with salt. Let cool.

4 Heat olive oil in a small skillet over medium. Cook onions, stirring occasionally, until browned, about 12 minutes.

5 Make the béchamel: Melt butter in a medium saucepan over medium. Add flour, and cook, whisking, 1 minute. Gradually whisk in milk, and cook, whisking, until mixture is thick and just starts to boil. Add ¼ cup blue cheese, the thyme, and 1 teaspoon salt, and whisk until cheese melts. Stir in cauliflower, half the onions, and half the chestnuts.

6 Spread cauliflower mixture into tart shell. Scatter remaining onions and chestnuts over filling, and dot top with remaining ¼ cup blue cheese. Bake tart on a baking sheet until golden on top and filling is bubbling, about 45 minutes. Let cool on a wire rack 15 minutes before cutting into pieces and serving.

Per serving: 281 calories, 20.7 g fat (11.23 g saturated fat), 45.99 mg cholesterol, 19.69 g carbohydrates, 5.66 g protein, 1.93 g fiber

California Veggie Sandwiches

These make-and-take sandwiches feature crisp raw vegetables and an easy herb-and-goat-cheese spread, for an appealing blend of tastes and textures: creamy, crunchy, tangy, and chewy. **SERVES 4**

8 ounces fresh goat cheese

¼ cup chopped fresh flat-leaf parsley

8 slices multi-grain bread, toasted

½ English cucumber, sliced

½ cup alfalfa sprouts

2 carrots, peeled and grated

¼ red onion, thinly sliced

2 large radishes, trimmed and cut into matchsticks

Coarse salt and freshly ground pepper

Mix goat cheese and parsley in a small bowl. Spread bread slices with goat cheese mixture. Layer 4 bread slices with cucumber, alfalfa sprouts, carrots, onion, and radish. Season with salt and pepper, sandwich with remaining bread slices, and serve.

Per serving: 337 calories, 14.55 g fat (8.81 g saturated fat), 26.08 mg cholesterol, 35.82 g carbohydrates, 17.74 g protein, 5.52 g fiber

Quinoa Veggie Burgers

The best veggie burgers taste like the vegetables, grains, and seeds from which they're made. This one does just that, drawing flavor and heft from mushrooms, zucchini, and quinoa. **SERVES 6**

2 portobello mushrooms (8 ounces), stemmed and cut into ½-inch pieces

1 small zucchini

¼ cup olive oil, plus more for brushing

1 large shallot, minced

¼ teaspoon crushed red pepper flakes

1 ounce finely grated Parmigiano-Reggiano (¼ cup)

2 cups cooked quinoa (see page 371)

Coarse salt and freshly ground pepper

1 large egg, lightly beaten

1½ cups fresh whole-wheat bread crumbs

Yogurt-Garlic Sauce (page 369)

6 whole-wheat buns, split and toasted

1 cup sprouts

½ English cucumber, sliced ¼ inch thick

1 Pulse mushrooms in a food processor until finely chopped; transfer to a bowl. Coarsely grate zucchini, place on paper towels, and squeeze to remove excess moisture. Add to mushrooms.

2 Heat 2 tablespoons olive oil in a large pan over medium. Add shallot and red pepper flakes, and cook until softened, about 2 minutes. Add mushrooms and zucchini, and cook until tender, about 2 minutes. Transfer to a bowl and add cheese and quinoa; season with salt and pepper. Let cool completely, then stir in egg and bread crumbs. Cover and refrigerate until firm, about 1 hour.

3 Heat remaining 2 tablespoons oil in a large nonstick skillet over medium. Shape mixture into six 1-inch-thick patties, pressing firmly. Cook in batches until golden brown, about 3 minutes per side. To serve, spread yogurt sauce onto buns and sandwich with patties, sprouts, and cucumber.

Per serving (with yogurt sauce): 496 calories, 21.28 g fat (4.2 g saturated fat), 41.28 mg cholesterol, 62.2 g carbohydrates, 17.36 g protein, 7.01 g fiber

Beans-and-Greens Tacos with Goat Cheese

Rethink taco night: Here, lightly toasted corn tortillas are filled with sautéed chard, red onions, and white beans and topped with crumbled goat cheese and cilantro. Vary the recipe by using other greens such as kale, spinach, or escarole, or swapping in black beans or pinto beans for the cannellini. **SERVES 4**

3 tablespoons olive oil

2 red onions, sliced into ¼-inch-thick rounds

5 garlic cloves, thinly sliced

1 pound Swiss chard, stems and ribs removed, leaves washed well and coarsely chopped

1 cup cooked cannellini beans (see page 365), drained and rinsed

½ cup vegetable stock, preferably homemade (see page 364)

Coarse salt and freshly ground pepper

8 white-corn tortillas (8-inch size)

⅓ cup crumbled fresh goat cheese (2 ounces)

Cilantro sprigs, for serving

1 Heat olive oil in a large high-sided skillet over medium. Cook onions until soft, stirring frequently, about 6 minutes. Add garlic, and cook, stirring, 1 minute. Stir in chard, beans, and stock. Cook until greens are wilted and beans are warmed through, about 4 minutes. Season with salt and pepper.

2 Using tongs, hold each tortilla directly over a gas flame, turning, until heated through, about 5 seconds. (Alternatively, wrap tortillas in parchment, then foil, and warm in a 350°F oven.) Spoon chard mixture onto tortillas, dividing evenly. Top with cheese and cilantro and serve.

G Per serving: 345 calories, 14.95 g fat (3.7 g saturated fat), 6.52 mg cholesterol, 44.64 g carbohydrates, 10.94 g protein, 8.01 g fiber

Grilled Asparagus and Ricotta Pizzas

A hot grill might just be the next best thing to a restaurant-quality wood-fired oven, giving the crust a wonderful crunch and a smoky flavor. **MAKES FOUR 10-INCH PIZZAS**

Extra-virgin olive oil, for grill and brushing

2 bunches asparagus, tough ends trimmed

All-purpose flour, for dusting

1 pound store-bought or homemade pizza dough (see page 267), divided into 4 equal pieces

Coarse salt and freshly ground pepper

1 cup part-skim ricotta cheese

¼ cup finely grated lemon zest

1. Heat grill to medium-high (see page 364), creating indirect heat on one side of grill. Clean and lightly oil hot grates. Grill asparagus until tender and browned in spots, about 5 minutes; transfer to a platter.

2. On a lightly floured work surface, stretch or roll each piece of dough into a 10-inch-long oval. Brush one side lightly with olive oil and season with salt and pepper. Using your hands, place dough shapes, oiled side down, directly over heat source. Brush dough with more olive oil and cook until underside is lightly charred and bubbles form all over top, 1 to 2 minutes. With tongs, flip dough and cook until lightly charred, 1 to 2 minutes. Slide dough to cooler side of grill.

3. Top crusts with ricotta and asparagus, dividing evenly; cover grill. Cook until asparagus and cheese are heated through, about 2 minutes. Sprinkle with lemon zest and serve warm.

Per pizza: 472 calories, 20.86 g fat (5.4 g saturated fat), 19.22 mg cholesterol, 52.28 g carbohydrates, 20.55 g protein, 10.02 g fiber

Double-Portobello Burgers with Roasted Tomatoes

The double-decker burger goes meat-free: two roasted portobello caps are better than one, especially when cheese is melted between them. Roasted plum tomatoes make a more healthful stand-in for ketchup. **MAKES 4**

- 8 portobello mushrooms, stemmed
- 2 tablespoons olive oil
- Coarse salt and freshly ground pepper
- 1 can (28 ounces) plum tomatoes, drained (reserve 3 tablespoons juice) and quartered lengthwise
- 5 garlic cloves, thinly sliced
- ⅛ teaspoon crushed red pepper flakes
- 2 ounces sharp provolone, grated
- 3 ounces arugula, washed and well drained
- 4 whole-wheat hamburger buns, split and toasted

1 Preheat oven to 450°F. Arrange mushrooms on a rimmed baking sheet, stem sides down, and brush with 1 tablespoon olive oil. Season with ¼ teaspoon salt and some pepper. On a second rimmed baking sheet lined with parchment, toss tomatoes with remaining tablespoon oil, the garlic, and red pepper flakes.

2 Roast vegetables, flipping mushrooms and stirring tomatoes halfway through, 25 minutes. Transfer tomatoes to a bowl, and toss with reserved juice.

3 Heat broiler, with rack 6 inches from heat source. Broil mushrooms 3 minutes. Flip, and top half the mushrooms with cheese, then with remaining mushrooms. Broil just until cheese melts, about 1 minute.

4 To serve, layer tomatoes, arugula, and mushrooms on bottom halves of buns, then sandwich with the top halves.

Per serving: 349 calories, 13.58 g fat (3.84 g saturated fat), 9.78 mg cholesterol, 47.95 g carbohydrates, 17.45 g protein, 10.28 g fiber

VERSATILE VEGETARIAN:
PIZZA

Making pizza from scratch is not hard to do, especially if you prepare the dough in advance. The addition of whole-wheat flour and toasted wheat germ yields a more wholesome dough. Our recipe makes enough for six thin-crust pies, allowing you to offer a variety of toppings so everyone can sample and share. Start with the tomato sauce, mozzarella, and basil combination in the margherita pie, then turn the page for more novel toppings.

LET DOUGH REST

SPREAD WITH SAUCE

ADD TOPPINGS

PIZZA MARGHERITA MAKES SIX 10- TO 12-INCH PIZZAS

Whole-Wheat Pizza
Dough (page 267)

All-purpose flour,
for dusting

Pizza Sauce (page 367)

16 ounces fresh mozzarella

Fresh basil leaves,
for garnish

1. Turn out dough onto a lightly floured surface. Cut dough into six equal portions. Roll into balls, cover with a clean kitchen towel, and let rest 30 minutes. To shape the dough, pat it flat with your hands; pick up the dough and rotate your hands around the edge to form it into a round. Place the dough over the tops of your knuckles, and pull gently to stretch it into a 10- to 12-inch round. Continue until dough is stretched very thin.

2. Preheat oven to 450°F, with a pizza stone or inverted baking sheet on rack in top third of oven. Working with one at a time, place dough round on a piece of parchment paper. Use a ladle to spread sauce (about ½ cup) on dough.

3. Arrange mozzarella on top of sauce, leaving space in between each slice. Transfer to oven by sliding parchment onto heated stone or baking sheet. Bake until cheese is bubbly and bottom of dough is crisp, 13 to 15 minutes. Serve immediately, garnished with basil.

Per serving (½ pizza): 392 calories, 15.67 g fat (6.91 g saturated fat), 26.77 mg cholesterol, 45.82 g carbohydrates, 17.44 g protein, 5.85 g fiber

WHOLE-WHEAT PIZZA DOUGH MAKES 3 POUNDS

1 envelope active dry yeast (1 scant tablespoon)

2 cups warm water (110°F)

2½ cups all-purpose flour, plus more for dusting

2 teaspoons coarse salt

2 cups whole-wheat flour

½ cup toasted wheat germ

Olive oil, for bowl

1. In a large bowl, dissolve yeast in the warm water and let stand 5 minutes. Stir in 2 cups all-purpose flour and the salt, then stir in whole-wheat flour, toasted wheat germ, and remaining ½ cup all-purpose flour, 1 tablespoon at a time, until dough comes away from the bowl but is still sticky.

2. Turn out onto a lightly floured work surface, and knead until dough is smooth and elastic and springs back slowly when pressed, about 10 minutes. Lightly oil a large bowl. Add dough, and turn to coat. Cover, and let rise in a warm place until it doubles in volume, about 2½ hours.

Fresh Tomato, Yellow Bell Pepper, and Red Onion Pizza

MAKES SIX 10-TO 12-INCH PIZZAS

Follow steps 1 and 2 of Pizza Margherita recipe (page 264). Dot each dough round with 2 teaspoons chopped GARLIC, ¼ cup thinly sliced RED ONION, ¼ cup thinly sliced YELLOW BELL PEPPER, ¼ cup halved CHERRY TOMATOES, 1 tablespoon small fresh BASIL leaves, and ½ cup mixed grated MOZZARELLA, FONTINA, and PARMESAN. Season with SALT and PEPPER, drizzle with OLIVE OIL, and bake as directed.

Per serving (½ pizza): 390 calories, 14.15 g fat (5.04 g saturated fat), 21.3 mg cholesterol, 48.5 g carbohydrates, 16.19 g protein, 6.31 g fiber

Pesto Pizza with Sunny-Side-Up Egg

MAKES SIX 10-TO 12-INCH PIZZAS

Follow steps 1 and 2 of Pizza Margherita recipe (page 264), omitting pizza sauce. Dot each dough round with ¼ cup PESTO (page 369), then top with ¼ cup chopped SCALLION and ½ cup mixed grated MOZZARELLA, FONTINA, and PARMESAN. Bake 10 minutes. Remove from oven and crack

1 large EGG on top of each pizza, season with SALT and PEPPER, and bake until egg white sets and yolk is slightly runny, about 5 minutes more.

Per serving (½ pizza): 556 calories, 33.36 g fat (9.18 g saturated fat), 135.85 mg cholesterol, 43.05 g carbohydrates, 23.37 g protein, 5.64 g fiber

Mushroom and Leek Pizza

MAKES SIX 10-TO 12-INCH PIZZAS

Heat 2 tablespoons OLIVE OIL in a medium skillet over medium. Add 1 LEEK, thinly sliced crosswise (well washed and drained), and 1 thinly sliced GARLIC CLOVE; cook until tender, stirring frequently, about 4 minutes. Increase heat to medium-high, add 2 cups (5 ounces) sliced WHITE MUSHROOMS, and cook, stirring, until tender, about 2 minutes more. Season with SALT. Follow step 1 of Pizza Margherita recipe (page 264), omitting pizza sauce. Dividing evenly among dough rounds, spread with ¾ cup PART-SKIM RICOTTA, drizzle with OLIVE OIL, and top with mushroom mixture. Bake as directed. Sprinkle with CRUSHED RED PEPPER FLAKES.

Per serving (½ pizza): 263 calories, 8.1 g fat (1.74 g saturated fat), 4.8 mg cholesterol, 39.49 g carbohydrates, 9.51 g protein, 4.36 g fiber

pasta and other noodles

Fettuccine with Parsley-Walnut Pesto

For best results, save some of the pasta cooking water for tossing with the noodles so the pesto coats them evenly, and add the baby spinach at the end so the leaves just wilt. **SERVES 4**

12 ounces fettuccine, preferably whole-wheat

Coarse salt and freshly ground pepper

2 cups packed fresh flat-leaf parsley leaves

¼ cup walnuts, plus more coarsely chopped for serving

1 ounce grated Parmigiano-Reggiano (¼ cup), plus more for serving

1 garlic clove

1 tablespoon fresh lemon juice

2 tablespoons water

¼ cup extra-virgin olive oil

5 ounces baby spinach

Pinch of crushed red pepper flakes

1. Cook pasta in a pot of boiling salted water until al dente, according to package directions. Reserve ½ cup pasta water; drain pasta, and return to pot.

2. Meanwhile, in a food processor, puree parsley, whole walnuts, cheese, garlic, lemon juice, and the water until a paste forms. With machine running, add olive oil in a thin stream; process until very smooth, about 1 minute. Season pesto with salt and pepper.

3. Add pesto, ¼ cup pasta water, and spinach to pasta in pot; toss to combine. Thin with more pasta water as needed. Serve sprinkled with chopped walnuts, cheese, and red pepper flakes.

Per serving: 513 calories, 20.3 g fat (3.5 g saturated fat), 6.24 mg cholesterol, 69.7 g carbohydrates, 15.8 g protein, 5.3 g fiber

Penne with Oven-Roasted Puttanesca Sauce

Cooking the tomato mixture in the oven involves much less stirring than traditional stovetop sauces. This complex-tasting puttanesca is a particularly good match for gluten-free pasta, and still pairs nicely with traditional varieties. **SERVES 6**

- 6 tomatoes (about 1¾ pounds), cut into 1-inch wedges
- 2 garlic cloves, thinly sliced
- 3 tablespoons capers, rinsed
- 2 tablespoons extra-virgin olive oil, plus more for drizzling

  Coarse salt and freshly ground pepper
- ⅓ cup pitted kalamata olives, halved
- 12 ounces gluten-free penne (brown rice, quinoa, or lentil)

1 Preheat oven to 425°F. Toss tomatoes, garlic, capers, olive oil, and a sprinkling of salt and pepper on a rimmed baking sheet. Roast 35 minutes, then reduce oven temperature to 375°F. Add olives, stirring once, and roast 15 minutes more.

2 Meanwhile, cook pasta in a pot of boiling salted water until al dente, according to package instructions. Drain.

3 Toss pasta with tomato sauce, and season with salt and pepper. Serve drizzled with more oil.

Ⓥ Ⓖ Ⓢ Per serving: 294 calories, 7 g fat (1 g saturated fat), 0 mg cholesterol, 51 g carbohydrates, 6 g protein, 3 g fiber

Spaghetti with Garlic and Herbs

Sometimes simple is best for pasta dishes. This whole-wheat spaghetti has only a few supporting ingredients: peperoncini, garlic (cooked and raw), parsley, and Parmigiano-Reggiano. **SERVES 2**

8 ounces whole-wheat spaghetti

Coarse salt and freshly ground pepper

1 tablespoon olive oil, plus more for drizzling

6 peperoncini, sliced into rings

6 to 8 garlic cloves, minced (2 tablespoons)

¾ cup chopped fresh flat-leaf parsley or basil, or a combination

½ cup (2 ounces) grated Parmigiano-Reggiano, plus more for serving

1. Cook pasta in a pot of boiling salted water until al dente, according to package instructions.

2. Just before pasta is finished cooking, heat olive oil over medium in a large skillet. Add peperoncini and half the garlic; toss and cook until heated through, 1 to 2 minutes.

3. Reserve 1 cup of pasta water, then drain pasta. Add pasta to skillet and stir to combine. Add just enough reserved pasta water to moisten; stir in remaining garlic and the herbs. Stir in cheese, then season with salt and pepper. Drizzle with more oil and sprinkle with more cheese, if desired, and serve.

Per serving: 288.3 calories, 7.15 g fat (2.36 g saturated fat), 8.8 mg cholesterol, 46.65 g carbohydrates, 12.86 g protein, 7.7 g fiber

Maltagliati with Marinated Heirloom Tomatoes

The first step in this nearly no-cook sauce is to gently heat garlic in olive oil, which is then used to marinate heirloom tomato wedges. Tossing the still-warm pasta with the tomatoes allows the flavors to meld better. **SERVES 8**

- 5 garlic cloves, thinly sliced
- ½ cup olive oil
- 2 pounds heirloom tomatoes, sliced into ½-inch wedges
- ¾ cup torn fresh basil leaves
- 3 tablespoons salt-packed capers, preferably Sicilian, rinsed, drained, and chopped if large
- 2 teaspoons finely grated lemon zest, plus more for sprinkling
- ¼ teaspoon crushed red pepper flakes
- Coarse salt and freshly ground pepper
- 1 pound maltagliati or other flat pasta, such as croxetti or pappardelle, preferably whole-wheat

1 Combine garlic and olive oil in a saucepan over low and cook until pale golden, about 10 minutes. Strain; reserve garlic oil and slivers. Let cool.

2 Combine tomatoes, ¼ cup basil, the capers, lemon zest, red pepper flakes, and ½ teaspoon salt in a large bowl. Pour garlic oil and slivers over tomato mixture. Cover and marinate, tossing occasionally, 30 minutes.

3 Meanwhile, cook pasta in a pot of boiling salted water until al dente, according to package instructions. Drain.

4 Add warm pasta to bowl, and toss gently. Top with remaining ½ cup basil. Season with pepper, sprinkle with lemon zest, and serve.

V Per serving: 342 calories, 14.59 g fat (2.05 g saturated fat), 0 mg cholesterol, 47.97 g carbohydrates, 9.6 g protein, 8.87 g fiber

Two-Bean Pasta Salad

Because you can make it up to a day ahead, this bean-and-pasta salad is great for casual summer entertaining. Even better: the flavors improve as the salad marinates in the refrigerator. **SERVES 4**

10 ounces green beans, trimmed and cut into 1-inch pieces (about 2½ cups)

Coarse salt and freshly ground pepper

8 ounces pasta shells, preferably whole-wheat, kamut, or spelt

¼ cup white balsamic or apple cider vinegar

1 teaspoon minced garlic

¼ teaspoon sugar (optional)

⅓ cup extra-virgin olive oil

2 celery stalks, cut crosswise into ⅛-inch slices (about 1 cup)

1 cup cooked black-eyed peas, kidney beans, or chickpeas (see page 365), drained and rinsed

½ cup shredded fresh basil leaves, plus more for garnish

1 Blanch green beans in a pot of boiling salted water until tender and bright green, about 3 minutes. Transfer to a colander with a slotted spoon and rinse under cold water to stop the cooking.

2 Add pasta to pot of boiling water and cook until al dente, according to package instructions. Drain and rinse under cold water.

3 In a large bowl, whisk together vinegar, garlic, ½ teaspoon salt, and the sugar, if using. Whisk in the olive oil in a steady stream, and season with pepper.

4 Add celery, black-eyed peas, and green beans to the vinaigrette, then add pasta and toss well to combine. Cover and let pasta salad marinate at least 1 hour and up to 1 day in the refrigerator.

5 Just before serving, stir in shredded basil, season with salt and pepper, and garnish with basil leaves.

V Per serving: 433 calories, 19 g fat (3 g saturated fat), 0 mg cholesterol, 57 g carbohydrates, 13 g protein, 10 g fiber

Pasta with Radicchio, Raisins, and Pine Nuts

Raisins and pine nuts are staples in Sicilian cooking; here they are sautéed with garlic to make a sauce for whole-grain pasta. Don't underestimate the creamy ricotta and shredded radicchio toppings; they are integral to the flavor of the whole dish. **SERVES 4**

8 ounces whole-grain pasta, such as spelt or farro

Coarse salt and freshly ground pepper

3 tablespoons extra-virgin olive oil

5 garlic cloves, minced (about 1 tablespoon)

⅔ cup golden raisins, coarsely chopped

½ cup toasted pine nuts (see page 363)

1 ounce grated Pecorino Romano (about ½ cup)

½ cup part-skim ricotta

½ head radicchio, cored and very thinly shredded (about 2 cups)

1 Cook pasta in a pot of boiling salted water until al dente, according to package instructions.

2 While pasta is cooking, heat olive oil in a large, straight-sided skillet over medium-high heat. Add garlic and raisins, and cook until fragrant, stirring frequently, about 2 minutes. Stir in pine nuts.

3 Drain pasta, reserving ½ cup pasta water. Add pasta to skillet, tossing to combine. Add enough pasta water to create a creamy sauce. Stir in half the Pecorino, and season with salt and pepper.

4 Divide pasta among 4 bowls. Top with ricotta, radicchio, and remaining Pecorino, and serve.

Per serving: 579 calories, 30.79 g fat (5.65 g saturated fat), 15.85 mg cholesterol, 61.66 g carbohydrates, 19.08 g protein, 9.95 g fiber

Pasta with Beet Greens, Blue Cheese, and Hazelnuts

A favorite salad trio—greens, cheese, and nuts—makes an unexpectedly delicious pasta topping. Mild-tasting beet greens go well with the more robust flavors of Gorgonzola and hazelnuts; kale, spinach, or Swiss chard are other options. To make use of the whole vegetable, use the beet roots in the salad on page 219. **SERVES 4**

12 ounces linguine, preferably whole-wheat

Coarse salt and freshly ground pepper

1 tablespoon extra-virgin olive oil, plus more for drizzling

1 garlic clove, minced

Greens from 2 bunches beets (about ½ pound), rinsed, tough stems removed, and coarsely chopped

⅓ cup toasted, skinned hazelnuts (see page 363), coarsely chopped

2 ounces blue cheese, such as Gorgonzola, crumbled

1. Cook pasta in a pot of boiling salted water until al dente, according to package instructions. Reserve ½ cup pasta water; drain pasta.

2. Meanwhile, in a large skillet, heat 1 tablespoon olive oil over medium-high. Add garlic and cook until fragrant, stirring, 30 seconds. Add greens and cook, stirring, until tender, 2 minutes.

3. Add pasta and hazelnuts; toss to combine. Add cheese and toss, adding enough pasta water to create a creamy sauce. Drizzle with olive oil, season with pepper, and serve.

Per serving: 505 calories, 18.2 g fat (4.4 g saturated fat), 10.63 mg cholesterol, 70 g carbohydrates, 18.3 g protein, 7.3 g fiber

Orzo Salad with Roasted Carrots and Dill

Picnics and potlucks call for portable salads. This deceptively delicious example features earthy roasted carrots and garlic along with bright lemon and dill. **SERVES 8 TO 10**

3 pounds carrots (about 4 bunches)

4 garlic cloves (unpeeled)

¼ cup extra-virgin olive oil

Coarse salt and freshly ground pepper

1 pound orzo, preferably whole-wheat

Grated zest and juice of 2 lemons

4 scallions, white and light-green parts, coarsely chopped

½ cup loosely packed fresh dill, coarsely chopped

1 Preheat oven to 450°F, with a rack in lower shelf. Cut carrots diagonally into 2-inch pieces. Toss carrots and garlic with 2 tablespoons olive oil and a pinch of salt. Divide among 2 rimmed baking sheets and arrange in an even layer. Roast until carrots are tender and browned, about 15 minutes. Let cool. Squeeze garlic cloves from skins; mince to form a coarse paste.

2 Cook pasta in a pot of boiling salted water until al dente, according to package instructions. Drain. While still hot, transfer orzo to a large bowl, and toss with remaining 2 tablespoons oil. Let cool slightly, and add roasted carrots.

3 Meanwhile, in a small bowl, mix together lemon zest, lemon juice, scallions, and roasted garlic. Add dill, and pour mixture over orzo mixture. Stir to combine; season with salt and pepper. If not serving immediately, cover and refrigerate up to 1 day; bring to room temperature before serving.

V Per serving (for 8 servings): 348.41 calories, 8.24 g fat (1.28 g saturated fat), 0.01 mg cholesterol, 61 g carbohydrates, 9.68 g protein, 6.97 g fiber

Soba and Tofu in Ginger Broth

Soba noodles, made from buckwheat, are a protein-rich option for making Asian dishes. This one includes a delicate broth and grilled tofu; the tofu can be broiled for about five minutes on each side instead of grilled. **SERVES 4**

6 scallions, whites and greens separated, greens cut into 2-inch lengths and thinly sliced lengthwise

1 piece (3 inches) fresh ginger, peeled and thinly sliced

2 garlic cloves, smashed

¼ cup low-sodium soy sauce, plus more if needed

1 tablespoon rice vinegar (unseasoned)

Canola oil, for grill pan

14 ounces extra-firm tofu, drained and pressed (see page 363)

Coarse salt and freshly ground pepper

6 ounces soba noodles

1 head baby bok choy, thinly sliced

4 ounces snow peas, trimmed and halved

1 fresh red chile, thinly sliced

1 teaspoon black sesame seeds, for garnish

1 In a medium saucepan, combine scallion whites, ginger, garlic, soy sauce, rice vinegar, and 8 cups water; bring to a boil. Cover and reduce to a simmer. Cook until flavorful, about 10 minutes.

2 Meanwhile, heat a grill pan over medium-high; lightly oil. Slice tofu in half crosswise; season with salt and pepper. Add tofu pieces to hot pan and cook, turning to grill all sides, about 15 minutes total. Remove from pan; once cool enough to handle, cut into small cubes.

3 Remove solids from broth with a slotted spoon; discard. Bring broth to a boil. Cook soba noodles in the broth until tender according to package directions. About 1 minute before the end of cooking, add bok choy, snow peas, and chile. Cook until vegetables are crisp-tender. Add more soy sauce, if desired. To serve, divide noodles and broth among 4 bowls; top with tofu, scallion greens, and sesame seeds.

Ⓥ Per serving: 269 calories, 6.18 g fat (1.04 g saturated fat), 0 mg cholesterol, 41.74 g carbohydrates, 17.24 g protein, 2.89 g fiber

Spinach Gnudi with Sage Butter

These beautiful green Italian dumplings are similar to gnocchi, or potato dumplings, but with spinach and ricotta in the dough. Brown butter flavored with sage is a traditional finish for gnocchi (and gnudi); it's so rich and nutty, a little goes a long way (only one tablespoon per serving). **SERVES 4**

1½ pounds spinach, large stems removed, washed well

2 large egg yolks, lightly beaten

¾ cup part-skim ricotta (about 6 ounces), drained for 30 minutes in a fine sieve

3 ounces (¾ cup) finely grated Parmigiano-Reggiano

1 cup plus 2 tablespoons all-purpose flour, plus more for hands

½ teaspoon freshly grated nutmeg

Coarse salt and freshly ground pepper

Semolina, for dusting

4 tablespoons (½ stick) unsalted butter

2 tablespoons coarsely chopped fresh sage leaves, plus about 8 whole leaves

1 Fill a large pot with 2 inches of water and bring to a simmer. Fit with a steamer basket or colander. Add spinach to basket, cover, and steam until bright green, 3 to 5 minutes. Drain, and let cool slightly. Press to remove liquid. Roll spinach in a clean kitchen towel or cheesecloth, and squeeze to remove any remaining liquid. Transfer to a food processor, and puree until smooth (you should have 1 scant cup).

2 Stir together spinach puree, egg yolks, both cheeses, 2 tablespoons flour, the nutmeg, 1 teaspoon salt, and pepper to taste in a bowl.

3 Mound remaining 1 cup flour on a cutting board. Using floured hands, gently shape 1 tablespoon spinach mixture into a small log. Drop it into the flour, and quickly roll to coat lightly. Transfer to a baking sheet that's lightly dusted with semolina. Repeat with remaining spinach mixture. Refrigerate, uncovered, until ready to cook (up to overnight).

4 Cook gnudi in a pot of boiling salted water, in two batches, until they rise to, and remain on, the surface, about 5 minutes.

5 Meanwhile, warm 4 plates. Melt butter in a small skillet over medium-high heat. Stir in chopped sage and the sage leaves. Add 1½ tablespoons gnudi cooking water, reduce heat to low, and cook until butter is golden brown, about 5 minutes. Season with salt and pepper, and cover to keep warm.

6 Use a slotted spoon to remove gnudi from water; shake off excess water, and transfer to warm plates. Drizzle with sage butter and serve.

Per serving: 456 calories, 24.51 g fat (14.15 g saturated fat), 165.65 mg cholesterol, 37.56 g carbohydrates, 23.59 g protein, 4.78 g fiber

No-Bake Lasagna with Ricotta and Tomatoes

In this twist on traditional lasagna, boiled noodles are tossed in a quick fresh-tomato sauce and then each serving is topped with two types of cheese—all without having to turn on the oven. **SERVES 4**

1 tablespoon plus 1 teaspoon olive oil

7 garlic cloves, thinly sliced

3 cups mixed red and yellow cherry or grape tomatoes, halved (2 pints)

Coarse salt and freshly ground pepper

⅔ cup vegetable stock, preferably homemade (see page 364)

8 lasagna noodles, preferably whole-wheat

⅔ cup small fresh basil leaves

½ cup part-skim ricotta

1 ounce Pecorino Romano, shaved

1. Heat 1 tablespoon olive oil in a high-sided skillet over medium. Cook garlic until pale golden, stirring, about 3 minutes. Add 2 cups tomatoes and season with salt. Cook until tomatoes are soft, about 7 minutes. Add stock. Simmer for 1 minute. Add remaining tomatoes and cook until warmed through, 1 to 2 minutes.

2. Meanwhile, cook pasta in a pot of boiling salted water until al dente, according to package instructions. Drain. Add pasta to skillet and toss to coat with sauce. Stir in basil, reserving some for garnish.

3. Divide pasta among 4 plates. Top with any remaining sauce. Dot with ricotta, and drizzle with remaining teaspoon oil. Top with shaved cheese and remaining basil. Sprinkle with pepper and serve.

Per serving: 357 calories, 10 g fat (3 g saturated fat), 15 mg cholesterol, 52 g carbohydrates, 16 g protein, 4 g fiber

Linguine with Toasted Almonds, Parsley, and Lemon

Almonds, parsley, lemon, and cheese—the makings of a delicious pesto—can also simply be tossed with pasta for an ultra-easy dish. Almond oil is used in this recipe; you can also drizzle it on vegetables after roasting, or whisk it into vinaigrettes. **SERVES 4**

8 ounces linguine, preferably whole-wheat

Coarse salt and freshly ground pepper

1 cup almonds, toasted (see page 363) and chopped

1 cup fresh flat-leaf parsley leaves, chopped

Grated zest and juice of 1 lemon

2 tablespoons almond oil or extra-virgin olive oil

¼ cup grated Pecorino Romano (½ ounce), for serving

1 Cook pasta in a pot of boiling salted water until al dente, according to package instructions. Reserve 1 cup pasta water, drain pasta.

2 Toss pasta with almonds, parsley, lemon zest and juice, and oil in a large bowl. Adjust consistency with reserved pasta water as desired. Season with salt and pepper, and serve with cheese.

Per serving: 492 calories, 26 g fat (3 g saturated fat), 4.4 mg cholesterol, 51 g carbohydrates, 15.76 g protein, 10.54 g fiber

Pasta with Roasted Pumpkin

Pumpkin, which is relatively high in protein and fiber, takes center stage in this vegetarian meal. Roasting brings out its natural sweetness; here it is helped along with a little honey before being tossed with nutty whole-grain pasta. **SERVES 4**

½ small sugar pumpkin, peeled, seeded, and cut into 1-inch chunks (about 4 cups)

¼ cup extra-virgin olive oil, plus more for drizzling

Coarse salt and freshly ground pepper

2 tablespoons honey

8 ounces whole-grain pasta, such as farro or spelt

2 teaspoons minced garlic

½ cup finely chopped toasted walnuts (see page 363)

¼ cup chopped fresh flat-leaf parsley leaves, plus sprigs for garnish

2 ounces finely grated Parmigiano-Reggiano (½ cup)

1 Preheat oven to 425°F. Toss pumpkin with 2 tablespoons olive oil, ½ teaspoon salt, and the honey. Roast in a single layer on a rimmed baking sheet until tender, about 45 minutes.

2 Meanwhile, cook pasta in a pot of boiling salted water until al dente, according to package instructions.

3 While pasta is cooking, heat remaining 2 tablespoons oil and the garlic in a skillet over medium-high until fragrant, stirring, about 1 minute. Add walnuts and roasted pumpkin. Toss to combine and heat through.

4 Reserve 1 cup pasta water; drain pasta. In a large bowl, toss pasta with ½ cup pasta water and stir in the parsley and cheese; add more pasta water if necessary to create a creamy sauce. Season with salt and pepper, and drizzle with oil. Add walnut and pumpkin mixture, garnish with parsley sprigs, and serve.

Per serving: 521 calories, 26 g fat (5 g saturated fat), 11 mg cholesterol, 61 g carbohydrates, 16 g protein, 7 g fiber

Pasta with Beets and Ricotta

Whole-grain spaghetti turns garnet when tossed with a puree of beets and sun-dried tomatoes (which add subtle sweetness); toasted walnuts add nutrients and flavor to the dish. **SERVES 4**

1 pound red beets, trimmed and scrubbed

¼ cup olive oil, plus more for drizzling

Coarse salt

½ cup toasted walnuts (see page 363)

1 tablespoon chopped sun-dried tomatoes

Crushed red pepper flakes

12 ounces farro spaghetti

½ cup fresh ricotta

1 Preheat oven to 425°F. Drizzle beets with olive oil and season with salt. Wrap tightly in parchment, then foil and roast until tender, about 1 hour. Let cool slightly, then rub off skins with paper towels. Chop beets.

2 Pulse beets, walnuts, and tomatoes in a food processor until chopped. Season with salt and red pepper flakes.

3 Cook pasta in a pot of boiling salted water until al dente, according to package directions. Drain, reserving 1 cup water, and return to pot.

4 Toss pasta with beet mixture, adding enough pasta water to create a creamy sauce. To serve, divide among 4 bowls and top with ricotta, drizzle with oil, and sprinkle with red pepper flakes.

Per serving: 591 calories, 27 g fat (4 g saturated fat), 10 mg cholesterol, 75 g carbohydrates, 21 g protein, 13 g fiber

Long Life Noodles

In Japan, noodles symbolize longevity—hence the name given this traditional and ceremonial dish of soba and vegetables, which is served on New Year's Day for good luck. Look for kombu (dried kelp) at Asian markets or specialty grocers. **SERVES 6**

1 piece (4 inches) dried kombu, cleaned with a damp cloth

1 piece (4 inches) fresh ginger, peeled and thinly sliced

2 small garlic cloves, peeled and sliced

1 small bunch fresh cilantro (with stems)

10 cups water

2 tablespoons prepared wasabi, or to taste

½ pound soba noodles

Coarse salt

1 sweet potato, peeled and cut into strips

1 small daikon radish, peeled and cut into strips

2 cups baby tat soi leaves, stems removed, or baby spinach

2 tablespoons lime juice

Soy sauce

4 scallions, thinly sliced (about ⅓ cup)

1 In a large saucepan over high heat, bring kombu, ginger, garlic, cilantro, and the water to a boil. Immediately remove kombu with tongs; discard. Add wasabi, and stir. Reduce heat; simmer 45 minutes, or until broth is very flavorful. Strain broth through a fine sieve into a large saucepan.

2 Cook soba in a pot of boiling salted water until tender, according to package instructions. Drain.

3 Bring reserved broth to a simmer over medium heat. Adjust seasoning with salt. Add sweet potato and daikon; cook until softened, about 2 minutes. Add noodles; cook, stirring gently, until warmed through, about 1 minute. Add tat soi leaves; cook just until wilted, about 30 seconds. Remove from heat. Add lime juice and season with soy sauce. Dividing evenly, transfer noodles and vegetables to bowls; add broth and scallions.

V Per serving: 200 calories, 1.95 g fat (0 g saturated fat), 0 mg cholesterol, 40.96 g carbohydrates, 7.69 g protein, 1.98 g fiber

Pasta with Roasted Cauliflower and Lemon Zest

Perhaps the only way to improve upon roasted cauliflower and capers, a delicious Italian specialty, is to toss them with pasta. Because they can be easily rinsed, capers packed in salt are less salty tasting than those packed in brine; look for them at specialty food stores, Italian grocers, or in many supermarkets. **SERVES 4**

1 large head cauliflower (about 2 pounds), cut into small florets (about 7 cups)

1 red onion, cut into ¼-inch-thick slices

¼ cup capers, preferably packed in salt, rinsed

¼ cup olive oil

Coarse salt and freshly ground pepper

8 ounces orecchiette, preferably whole-wheat

½ cup coarsely chopped fresh flat-leaf parsley leaves

2 tablespoons finely grated lemon zest (from 2 lemons)

1. Preheat oven to 450°F. Toss together cauliflower, onion, capers, and 2 tablespoons olive oil on a rimmed baking sheet; season with salt and pepper. Spread vegetables in a single layer and roast, tossing halfway through, until cauliflower is tender and browned, about 40 minutes.

2. Meanwhile, cook pasta in a pot of boiling salted water until al dente, according to package instructions. Drain.

3. Toss hot pasta with remaining 2 tablespoons oil, the parsley, and lemon zest. Add cauliflower mixture, and season with salt and pepper. Gently toss to combine, and serve.

V Per serving: 389 calories, 14.68 g fat (2.1 g saturated fat), 0 mg cholesterol, 58.02 g carbohydrates, 13.51 g protein, 11.37 g fiber

Garden-Vegetable Linguine

Take a laid-back approach to summer pasta dishes by broiling a topping of just-picked vegetables—from the farmer's market or, if you're lucky, from your own garden. Almost any assortment will do; this version features tomatoes, chiles, fennel, and fresh basil. **SERVES 4**

1 large head fennel, quartered, cored, and sliced into ½-inch pieces

2 mild chiles, such as Anaheim or poblano (ribs and seeds removed for less heat, if desired), sliced into ½-inch pieces

1 pound cherry tomatoes

2 small red onions, sliced into ½-inch wedges

¼ cup plus 2 tablespoons olive oil

Coarse salt

10 ounces linguine, preferably whole-wheat

½ cup finely grated Parmigiano-Reggiano, plus more for serving

¾ cup fresh basil leaves

1 Heat broiler, with rack 4 inches from heat source. Arrange fennel and chiles on one rimmed baking sheet and tomatoes and onions on another. Toss each with 2 tablespoons olive oil and season with salt. Spread in a single layer and broil 3 minutes, then toss and continue broiling until vegetables are tender and charred in spots, about 2 minutes more. (Broil one sheet at a time if necessary.) Transfer vegetables and pan juices to a bowl.

2 Meanwhile, cook pasta in a pot of boiling salted water until al dente, according to package instructions. Reserve 1 cup pasta water, drain pasta, and return to pot.

3 Add vegetables, cheese, and reserved pasta water. Stir in basil and remaining 2 tablespoons oil and season with salt. Serve immediately, sprinkled with additional cheese.

Per serving: 539 calories, 27.94 g fat (5.21 g saturated fat), 8.8 mg cholesterol, 58.23 g carbohydrates, 17.49 g protein, 14.33 g fiber

Rice Noodles with Broccoli Pesto

Broccoli, basil, and almonds combine to make a no-cheese pesto for rice noodles, with some of the florets for a topping. Rice noodles are especially popular in Southeast Asian cooking, and offer a gluten-free alternative to traditional pasta; this recipe calls for medium noodles, also called rice sticks, rice fettuccine, or *banh pho*. **SERVES 4**

1 head broccoli (about 1 pound), cut into florets, stems sliced

Coarse salt and freshly ground pepper

¼ cup plus 2 tablespoons sliced toasted almonds (see page 363), plus more for garnish

¼ cup fresh basil leaves, plus small leaves for garnish

1 garlic clove, minced

2 tablespoons fresh lemon juice

¼ cup plus 2 tablespoons extra-virgin olive oil

8 ounces medium rice noodles

1 Blanch broccoli in a pot of boiling salted water until bright green and just tender, about 2 minutes. Remove with a slotted spoon, season with salt, and let cool slightly. Reserve water.

2 Coarsely chop 1 cup cooked florets. Puree remaining florets with the almonds, basil, garlic, and lemon juice in a food processor. Add olive oil and puree to combine. Season with salt and pepper.

3 Return water to a boil and cook rice noodles until tender according to package instructions. Reserve 1 cup cooking water, drain noodles, and return to pot. Toss with pesto, adding enough reserved pasta water to create a creamy sauce. Top each bowl with chopped florets, small basil leaves, and sliced almonds. Season with pepper and serve.

V **G** Per serving: 512 calories, 28 g fat (3 g saturated fat), 0 mg cholesterol, 60.07 g carbohydrates, 10 g protein, 6 g fiber

Golden-Tomato and Kale Pasta

Here's a neat trick for preparing pasta dishes with vegetables: the kale is blanched just until tender and bright green during the last minute of the pasta cooking time. You could use this same method with spinach, Swiss chard, asparagus, or snap peas, among other vegetables. Sautéed Sun Gold tomatoes add bursts of color and sweetness to the dish, which is finished with ricotta, a drizzle of olive oil, and a sprinkle of chile flakes. **SERVES 4**

2 tablespoons olive oil, plus more for drizzling

2 garlic cloves, sliced

1 pound golden cherry tomatoes

Coarse salt

12 ounces whole-wheat fettuccine

1 bunch kale (1 pound) stems removed, leaves torn into 2-inch pieces

½ cup part-skim ricotta

Crushed red pepper flakes

1 Heat oil in a large sauté pan over medium heat. Add garlic and tomatoes and cook, stirring, until tomatoes begin to burst, about 8 minutes. Season with salt.

2 Meanwhile, cook pasta in a pot of boiling salted water until al dente, according to package directions. Add kale during the last minute of cooking. Reserve some pasta water and drain pasta and kale. Return pasta and kale to pot and stir in sautéed tomatoes. Add reserved pasta water to adjust the consistency.

3 Divide into 4 bowls and top each with a dollop of ricotta. Drizzle ricotta with oil and season with salt and red pepper flakes.

Per serving: 491 calories, 11.42 g fat (2.94 g saturated fat), 9.62 mg cholesterol, 81.24 g carbohydrates, 19.93 g protein, 6.35 g fiber

VERSATILE VEGETARIAN:
PESTO

Pesto in its classic form (see page 369) is a sensational sauce, but you can also make a variety of pestos from different vegetables, herbs, and other flavorings. Leafy greens such as broccoli rabe, spinach, and arugula are used in the recipes that follow, as are roasted bell peppers and chipotle chiles in a smoky red version. And because these vegetables add plenty of bulk, you don't need as much oil and cheese to achieve the right texture. Practically any type of nut will work, from traditional pine nuts and walnuts to almonds and hazelnuts. Besides being tossed with pasta, these pestos make excellent crostini toppings, sandwich spreads, soup garnishes, or salad dressings, thinned with a little water.

BLANCH GREENS

PROCESS INGREDIENTS

ADD OIL AND FINISH

BROCCOLI RABE PESTO MAKES ABOUT 2 CUPS

1 bunch broccoli rabe (about 1 pound), tough stems removed

Coarse salt

⅓ cup toasted pine nuts (see page 363)

⅓ cup finely grated Parmigiano-Reggiano

¼ teaspoon crushed red pepper flakes

⅓ cup extra-virgin olive oil

1. Prepare a large ice-water bath. Blanch the broccoli rabe in a pot of boiling salted water until bright green and just tender, about 1 minute. Transfer broccoli rabe to the ice bath and let cool completely. Drain well in a colander.

2. Combine broccoli rabe, pine nuts, grated cheese, and the red pepper flakes in a food processor. Pulse until mixture is coarsely chopped.

3. Drizzle in the olive oil and process until smooth. Season with salt. Pesto can be refrigerated in a covered container up to 3 days.

G Per serving (for 8 servings): 165 calories, 14.53 g fat (2.19 g saturated fat), 2.93 mg cholesterol, 3.45 g carbohydrates, 4.63 g protein, 1.9 g fiber

WALNUT-SAGE PESTO

SMOKY BELL PEPPER PESTO

NUT-FREE ARUGULA PESTO

ALMOND-MINT PESTO

SPINACH-BASIL PESTO

Walnut-Sage Pesto   MAKES 1 CUP

In a food processor, pulse 2 chopped GARLIC CLOVES, 2 cups flat-leaf PARSLEY leaves, and ¼ cup SAGE leaves; process until combined. Add ½ cup toasted WALNUTS (see page 363) and 2 tablespoons toasted PINE NUTS (see page 363); pulse until finely chopped. With motor running, pour ½ cup EXTRA-VIRGIN OLIVE OIL through the feed tube in a slow, steady stream. Add ½ cup grated PARMIGIANO-REGGIANO; pulse to combine. Season with SALT and PEPPER.

G Per serving (2 tablespoons): 205 calories, 21.01 g fat (3.31 g saturated fat), 4.4 mg cholesterol, 1.74 g carbohydrates, 3.25 g protein, 0.51 g fiber

Smoky Bell Pepper Pesto   MAKES 1¼ CUPS

In a food processor, pulse 2 large roasted BELL PEPPERS (see page 364), 1 chopped jarred CHIPOTLE CHILE in adobo, 1 chopped small GARLIC CLOVE, 2 tablespoons toasted ALMONDS (see page 363), and 1 teaspoon fresh OREGANO leaves until coarsely chopped. Drizzle in 2 tablespoons EXTRA-VIRGIN OLIVE OIL and process until combined. Season with SALT and PEPPER.

V G Per serving (2 tablespoons): 44 calories, 3.83 g fat (0.48 g saturated fat), 0 mg cholesterol, 2 g carbohydrates, 0.64 g protein, 0.8 g fiber

Almond-Mint Pesto   MAKES ½ CUP

Process 1 ounce (about ¼ cup) chopped toasted blanched ALMONDS (see page 363) and 1 chopped SHALLOT in a food processor until a coarse paste forms. Add 1 cup loosely packed MINT leaves; pulse a few times until coarsely chopped. Add ½ cup grated PARMIGIANO-REGGIANO and 1 tablespoon plus 2 teaspoons EXTRA-VIRGIN OLIVE OIL; pulse a few times until combined. Season with SALT and PEPPER.

G Per serving (2 tablespoons): 195 calories, 19.06 g fat (3.11 g saturated fat), 4.4 mg cholesterol, 2.99 g carbohydrates, 3.74 g protein, 1.06 g fiber

Nut-Free Arugula Pesto   MAKES 1¼ CUPS

Combine 1 bunch trimmed and washed ARUGULA (about 4 ounces) and 4 peeled and smashed GARLIC CLOVES in a food processor; pulse until finely chopped, scraping down sides with a flexible spatula if necessary. Add 1 cup grated PARMIGIANO-REGGIANO (4 ounces) and ½ cup EXTRA-VIRGIN OLIVE OIL, and puree until smooth and well combined. Season with SALT and PEPPER.

G Per serving (2 tablespoons): 140 calories, 13.57 g fat (2.96 g saturated fat), 7.04 mg cholesterol, 1.13 g carbohydrates, 3.44 g protein, 0.2 g fiber

Spinach-Basil Pesto   MAKES ½ CUP

Heat 1 teaspoon EXTRA-VIRGIN OLIVE OIL in a medium skillet over medium. Add 1 sliced GARLIC CLOVE and cook until tender, but not browned, about 1 minute. Add 4 ounces BABY SPINACH and cook, stirring, until wilted and bright green, about 1 minute. Remove spinach from pan using a slotted spoon and let cool slightly. Squeeze out excess moisture from spinach, then pulse with ½ cup BASIL leaves, 1 tablespoon HAZELNUTS, toasted and skinned (see page 363), 2 tablespoons freshly grated PECORINO ROMANO, and 2 tablespoons EXTRA-VIRGIN OLIVE OIL in a food processor until combined. Season with SALT and PEPPER.

G Per serving (¼ cup): 174 calories, 17.18 g fat (2.65 g saturated fat), 2.2 mg cholesterol, 3.78 g carbohydrates, 2.04 g protein, 1.62 g fiber

simple side dishes

Green Beans with Hazelnuts and Gorgonzola

Steamed green beans make an elegant (and super simple) holiday dish when topped with crumbled blue cheese and toasted hazelnuts—a nice alternative to almonds, which are very often tossed with the beans. **SERVES 8**

2 pounds green beans, stem ends trimmed

2 tablespoons nut oil, such as hazelnut, almond, or walnut

1 tablespoon sherry vinegar

Coarse salt and freshly ground pepper

2 ounces Gorgonzola cheese, crumbled (about ½ cup)

½ cup blanched hazelnuts, toasted (see page 363) and coarsely chopped

1 Place a steamer basket or colander in a large pot filled with 1 inch of water, and bring to a rapid simmer. Lay green beans in steamer, spreading evenly, and cover pot; cook until beans are crisp-tender and bright green, 4 to 8 minutes.

2 Transfer beans to a bowl and toss with nut oil and vinegar; season with salt and pepper. Transfer to a platter, sprinkle with Gorgonzola and nuts, and serve.

ⓖ Per serving: 143 calories, 10 g fat (2 g saturated fat), 8 mg cholesterol, 9 g carbohydrates, 5 g protein, 4 g fiber

Grilled Potatoes with Garlic-Herb Oil

You might not think to grill potatoes, but it's a great method for cooking them, especially in summer. They need to be parboiled until tender first so they will cook through later. Here the potatoes are tossed in a simple garlic and herb oil after they come off the grill. Serve with your favorite vegetable burgers or egg dishes. **SERVES 4**

1½ pounds baby red potatoes
     Large-flake sea salt

3 tablespoons extra-virgin olive oil

¼ cup fresh flat-leaf parsley leaves, coarsely chopped

2 garlic cloves, finely grated

1 Heat grill to medium-high (see page 364). Place potatoes in a large pot, and fill with cold water. Season with salt, and bring to a boil. Reduce heat, and simmer until potatoes are just tender, 12 to 13 minutes. Drain, and let cool slightly. Halve potatoes, and toss with 1 tablespoon olive oil.

2 Meanwhile, whisk together parsley, garlic, and remaining 2 tablespoons oil in a large bowl.

3 Grill potatoes directly on grates, until slightly charred and crisp, 1 to 2 minutes per side. Toss with garlic-herb oil. Season with salt and serve.

Ⓥ Ⓖ Ⓢ Per serving: 217 calories, 10.78 g fat (1.53 g saturated fat), 0 mg cholesterol, 27.78 g carbohydrates, 3.42 g protein, 3.05 g fiber

Asparagus Mimosa

To make this dish, named for the pretty yellow-and-white flower, a peeled hard-cooked egg is pressed through a fine-mesh sieve to create a bright and fluffy topping for steamed asparagus. It's pitch-perfect for Easter—or any other springtime meal. **SERVES 4**

2 pounds asparagus, tough ends trimmed

1 tablespoon white-wine vinegar

2 teaspoons Dijon mustard

Coarse salt and freshly ground pepper

3 tablespoons extra-virgin olive oil

1 large egg, hard-cooked (see page 363)

1 Place a steamer basket in a large pot filled with 1 inch of water, and bring to a rapid simmer. Lay asparagus in steamer, spreading evenly, and cover pot; cook until asparagus is crisp-tender and bright green, about 5 minutes. Transfer asparagus to a serving platter.

2 Whisk together vinegar, mustard, ½ teaspoon coarse salt, and ¼ teaspoon pepper. Slowly whisk in olive oil. Push egg through a fine sieve. Spoon vinaigrette over asparagus, top with the egg, and serve.

Ⓖ Per serving: 167 calories, 12 g fat (2 g saturated fat), 53 mg cholesterol, 9.11 g carbohydrates, 6.56 g protein, 4.67 g fiber

Glazed Carrots with Whole Spices and Rosemary

Visit a farmer's market during spring to find carrots in an assortment of bright hues. These carrots are cooked in a mixture of vinegar, honey, and whole spices. The singular taste of star anise permeates (without overwhelming) the dish; pink peppercorns also lend a distinctive flavor, but white or black peppercorns can be substituted. **SERVES 4**

2 pounds slender carrots in assorted colors, with greens attached (or regular carrots, halved lengthwise)

Coarse salt

3 tablespoons packed light brown sugar

1 tablespoon plus 1 teaspoon white-wine vinegar

2 tablespoons honey

1 teaspoon whole pink peppercorns

2 tablespoons extra-virgin olive oil, plus more for drizzling (optional)

2 sprigs rosemary

1 whole star anise

1. Prepare an ice-water bath. Peel and trim carrots, leaving 1½ inches of greens intact. Blanch carrots in a large pot of boiling salted water until bright and crisp-tender, 3 to 4 minutes. Immediately plunge carrots into the ice bath to cool. Drain.

2. Preheat oven to 375°F. Whisk together brown sugar, vinegar, honey, and peppercorns.

3. Heat olive oil in a large ovenproof skillet over medium-high. Add carrots, rosemary, and star anise; cook, stirring, 5 minutes. Stir in honey mixture. Season with salt. Bring to a boil over medium-high heat, turning carrots to coat.

4. Transfer skillet to oven. Roast carrots until slightly caramelized, tossing once or twice, 20 to 25 minutes. Drizzle with olive oil, if desired, and serve.

G S Per serving: 229 calories, 7.6 g fat (1.07 g saturated fat), 0 mg cholesterol, 40.91 g carbohydrates, 2.19 g protein, 6.56 g fiber

Baked Polenta "Fries"

Creamy polenta offers a new way to make "fries." Pour polenta into an even layer in a pan (it will set as it cools), then slice into slender strips and bake. You could also use a store-bought tube of polenta instead of making your own. Serve with Tomato Sauce (page 367) as a more healthful alternative to ketchup. You could also sprinkle the fries with freshly grated Parmigiano-Reggiano and chopped fresh thyme or rosemary, or add a spice with a little heat instead. **SERVES 6**

  Basic Polenta (firm; page 366), cut into ¼- to ½-inch-thick strips
2 tablespoons olive oil
  Coarse salt and freshly ground pepper

Preheat oven to 450°F. On 2 rimmed baking sheets, drizzle polenta evenly with olive oil and season with salt and pepper; toss to combine, then spread in a single layer. Bake, rotating sheets halfway through, until polenta is golden and crisp, 35 to 40 minutes. Serve immediately.

V G S Per serving: 129 calories, 5 g fat (0.65 g saturated fat), 0 mg cholesterol, 18 g carbohydrates, 2 g protein, 1.33 g fiber

Zucchini and Feta Chopped Salad

Peak-of-the-season zucchini is delicious even when eaten raw, as in this refreshing salad. Look for a good-quality feta cheese from specialty grocers and cheese shops; French, Bulgarian, and Greek varieties are especially flavorful. This would be a nice side for a vegetable burger, or as part of an all-vegetable buffet in late summer. **SERVES 4**

1 zucchini, cut into ½-inch cubes
¾ cup crumbled feta cheese (3 ounces)
3 tablespoons extra-virgin olive oil
2 tablespoons small dill sprigs
  Thin strips lemon zest, plus 1 tablespoon plus 1 teaspoon fresh lemon juice
  Coarse salt and freshly ground pepper

Toss together zucchini, feta, olive oil, dill, and lemon juice. Season with salt and pepper. Sprinkle with lemon zest and serve.

G Per serving: 154 calories, 14.02 g fat (3.75 g saturated fat), 7.5 mg cholesterol, 3.91 g carbohydrates, 4.76 g protein, 0.91 g fiber

Mexican Creamed Corn

A favorite side dish takes on extra flavors: jalapeño chile, feta cheese (or queso fresco), and fresh cilantro. Yogurt makes a more healthful substitute for milk or cream, yet with just as much creaminess as in original versions. Serve it with vegetable tacos, chili, or Mexican-style rice and beans. **SERVES 4**

2 tablespoons olive oil

1 jalapeño chile, finely chopped (ribs and seeds removed for less heat, if desired)

1 shallot, finely chopped

4 ears corn, kernels and pulp scraped

1 cup water

½ cup plain low-fat yogurt

Coarse salt and freshly ground pepper

3 tablespoons crumbled feta cheese or queso fresco

2 tablespoons chopped fresh cilantro leaves

1 In a medium saucepan, heat olive oil over medium. Cook jalapeño and shallot, stirring, until softened, 2 to 3 minutes. Add corn kernels and pulp and the water. Cook, stirring, until corn is tender, 5 to 7 minutes.

2 Remove from heat, stir in yogurt, and season with salt and pepper. Serve immediately, topped with feta and cilantro.

G Per serving: 184 calories, 10 g fat (2 g saturated fat), 8 mg cholesterol, 21 g carbohydrates, 6 g protein, 3 g fiber

Tomato, Squash, and Potato Tian

This version of tian, a classic Provençal dish, incorporates potatoes in addition to more traditional tomatoes and summer squash. Plus, a hidden layer of sautéed onion serves as a flavor booster. Think of it as an easier, lighter gratin, with only a small amount of olive oil and cheese added to the assembled dish. **SERVES 8**

2 tablespoons extra-virgin olive oil, plus more for drizzling

1 onion, thinly sliced

2 small tomatoes, sliced ¼ inch thick

1 yellow summer squash, sliced ¼ inch thick

1 Yukon gold potato, sliced ¼ inch thick

Coarse salt and freshly ground pepper

1 tablespoon fresh thyme leaves

2 tablespoons freshly grated Parmigiano-Reggiano

1. Preheat oven to 375°F. Heat olive oil in a medium skillet over medium. Cook onion until tender and lightly golden, stirring frequently, 6 to 8 minutes.

2. Arrange the onion in an even layer on the bottom of a 9-by-13-inch baking dish. Layer tomato, squash, and potato on top of the onion, alternating the vegetables and overlapping slices slightly. Season with salt and pepper, sprinkle with thyme and cheese, and drizzle with oil.

3. Cover with parchment, then foil; bake 30 minutes. Uncover and bake until golden, 30 minutes more. Serve warm.

G Per serving: 62 calories, 4 g fat (1 g saturated fat), 1 mg cholesterol, 7 g carbohydrates, 2 g protein, 1 g fiber

Three Easy Salads

The following summer side dishes each feature just three main ingredients and minimal seasonings.

Grilled Corn, Avocado, and Cilantro Salad SERVES 4

- 4 ears corn, shucked
- 1 ripe but firm avocado, halved, pitted, peeled, and sliced
- ¼ cup fresh cilantro leaves
- 1 tablespoon fresh lime juice
- 1 tablespoon extra-virgin olive oil
  - Coarse salt

Heat grill to medium-high (see page 364). Grill corn, rotating often, until lightly charred, about 15 minutes. Let cool slightly. Cut kernels from cob. Toss with avocado, cilantro, lime juice, and oil; season with salt, and serve.

V G S Per serving: 163 calories, 8 g fat (1 g saturated fat), 0 mg cholesterol, 22 g carbohydrates, 4 g protein, 5 g fiber

Fennel, Snap Pea, and Tarragon Salad SERVES 4

- 1 fennel bulb, trimmed and quartered (core trimmed but left intact)
- 7 ounces sugar snap peas, thinly sliced
- 2 tablespoons chopped fresh tarragon
- 2 tablespoons fresh lemon juice
- 1 tablespoon extra-virgin olive oil
  - Coarse salt

Using a mandoline, slice fennel very thin. Toss with peas, tarragon, lemon juice, and oil; season with salt and serve.

V G S Per serving: 82 calories, 3 g fat (0 g saturated fat), 0 mg cholesterol, 9 g carbohydrates, 2 g protein, 3 g fiber

Potato Salad with Peas and Mint SERVES 4

- 1¼ pounds baby red potatoes
- ½ cup fresh or frozen peas
- 2 tablespoons extra-virgin olive oil
- ⅓ cup chopped fresh mint leaves
  - Coarse salt and freshly ground pepper

Place potatoes in a large saucepan and cover with water by 1 inch. Bring to a boil, then reduce heat and simmer until easily pierced with a fork, 11 to 14 minutes; drain. Halve potatoes.

Meanwhile, simmer peas in a saucepan of water until tender, about 4 minutes; drain, reserving ¼ cup cooking liquid. Using a fork, mash peas with 1 tablespoon olive oil and 2 tablespoons reserved cooking liquid. Gradually stir in remaining 2 tablespoons cooking liquid until mixture is thick and chunky.

Toss potatoes with pea mixture and mint leaves, then season with salt and pepper. Drizzle with remaining 1 tablespoon olive oil and serve.

V G S Per serving: 145 calories, 4 g fat (1 g saturated fat), 0 mg cholesterol, 25 g carbohydrates, 4 g protein, 4 g fiber

Broiled Zucchini with Yogurt Sauce

When an outdoor grill is not an option, use the broiler to achieve that same smoky flavor. Here, thick slices of zucchini are broiled and then drizzled with a zesty yogurt sauce. **SERVES 4**

2 tablespoons extra-virgin olive oil

4 zucchini, halved lengthwise

Coarse salt and freshly ground pepper

⅓ cup plain low-fat yogurt

1 tablespoon fresh lemon juice

¼ teaspoon ground coriander

¼ teaspoon ground mustard

¼ cup fresh cilantro leaves

1 Heat broiler with a rack 6 inches from heat source. On a rimmed baking sheet, toss zucchini with olive oil; arrange in a single layer, cut side up. Season with salt and pepper. Broil until zucchini are deep golden brown, 8 to 10 minutes.

2 Meanwhile, in a small bowl, stir together yogurt, lemon juice, coriander, and mustard. Season with salt and pepper.

3 Transfer zucchini to a serving platter, drizzle with yogurt sauce, and sprinkle with cilantro leaves.

G Per serving: 109 calories, 8 g fat (1 g saturated fat), 1.22 mg cholesterol, 8 g carbohydrates, 3 g protein, 2 g fiber

Tomatoes Provençal

A layer of golden bread crumbs makes a dish of juicy baked tomatoes all the more enticing. As in a classic French tian (see page 323), the tomatoes are seasoned with thyme; try them with basil or oregano for an Italian-flavored variation. **SERVES 4**

2 tablespoons extra-virgin olive oil, plus more for baking dish

¾ cup fresh plain bread crumbs (see page 363)

2 tablespoons finely grated Parmigiano-Reggiano

1 tablespoon fresh thyme leaves

Coarse salt and freshly ground pepper

4 large tomatoes, sliced ½ inch thick

1 Preheat oven to 400°F. Lightly oil a 2-quart baking dish or 4 ramekins (6 to 8 ounces). In a bowl, combine bread crumbs, cheese, thyme, and olive oil; season with salt and pepper.

2 Arrange tomatoes in prepared baking dish, overlapping slices slightly; season with salt and pepper. Top with bread crumb mixture. Bake until tomatoes are tender and crumbs are golden brown, 15 to 20 minutes. Serve immediately.

Per serving: 193 calories, 9.42 g fat (1.75 g saturated fat), 2.2 mg cholesterol, 23.35 g carbohydrates, 5.24 g protein, 3.04 g fiber

Mashed White Beans and Vegetables

Mashed potatoes head in a new, healthier direction, incorporating extra vegetables for well-rounded flavor and white beans for protein and a silky texture. There's no need for butter or cream—a small amount of olive oil does the trick—so it's vegan-friendly, too. The mash makes an utterly delicious base for garlicky broccoli rabe or slow-roasted tomatoes (see page 361), or as a topping for crostini or bruschetta, with or without Parmigiano-Reggiano shaved over the top. **SERVES 6**

2 tablespoons olive oil, plus more for drizzling

1 onion, coarsely chopped

1 celery stalk, thinly sliced

1 carrot, peeled and thinly sliced

2 pounds Yukon Gold potatoes, peeled and cut into 1-inch chunks

1½ cups cooked white beans (see page 365), drained and rinsed

Coarse salt and freshly ground pepper

1 Heat olive oil in a medium saucepan over medium. Cook onion, celery, and carrot until translucent, stirring frequently, 6 to 8 minutes. Add potatoes and white beans and cover with water by 2 inches. Bring to a boil, then season generously with salt. Reduce heat and simmer until potatoes are tender, about 8 minutes. Drain, reserving about 1 cup cooking liquid.

2 Mash vegetables and beans, adding reserved cooking liquid to adjust consistency. Season with salt and pepper, drizzle with oil, and serve.

Ⓥ Ⓖ Ⓢ Per serving: 206 calories, 5 g fat (1 g saturated fat), 0 mg cholesterol, 41 g carbohydrates, 9 g protein, 8 g fiber

Sautéed Kohlrabi with Onion and Cream

Part bulb, part bundle of greens, kohlrabi offers a delightful combination of familiar tastes; think of it as a cross between radish, collards, and broccoli, with the sweetness of jicama. Both the bulb and leaves are edible. If you have a young, tender kohlrabi, you won't need to peel the bulb; otherwise, remove the rough skin with a vegetable peeler. You can serve it raw—shredded into slaws or chopped into salads—or in a variety of simple cooking methods, including the one used here. **SERVES 4**

1¾ pounds kohlrabi with leaves attached

¼ cup water

2 tablespoons unsalted butter

½ cup thinly sliced onion

¼ cup heavy cream

Coarse salt and freshly ground pepper

1 Separate leaves from kohlrabi and finely slice to yield 3 cups; cut flesh into ½-inch cubes to yield 4 cups. Bring the water to a boil in a medium saucepan and add the kohlrabi cubes. Cover, reduce to a simmer, and cook until just tender, about 8 minutes.

2 Add butter and onion and simmer, stirring occasionally, until onion is tender, about 5 minutes. Stir in kohlrabi leaves and the cream and cook, stirring, until leaves are tender but still green, 3 to 5 minutes. Season with salt and pepper and serve immediately.

Ⓖ Per serving: 165 calories, 11.42 g fat (7.06 g saturated fat), 35.43 mg cholesterol, 14.93 g carbohydrates, 4.36 g protein, 8.16 g fiber

Broccolini with Lemon

Broccolini looks like baby broccoli, but it's actually a natural hybrid of broccoli and Chinese kale. The two-step cooking method used here (first blanch, then sauté in olive oil with lemon zest) would also work for other leafy greens like broccoli rabe and collards. Serve it over barley, quinoa, or polenta; toss with whole-grain pasta; or use it as a pizza topping. **SERVES 4**

- 1 pound broccolini (1 to 2 bunches)
  Coarse salt
- 2 teaspoons extra-virgin olive oil
  Zest (removed in long strips) and juice of ½ lemon

1 Prepare an ice-water bath. Blanch broccolini in a large pot of salted boiling water until tender, about 4 minutes. Transfer broccolini to the ice bath to cool. Drain and pat dry.

2 Heat olive oil in a large high-sided skillet over medium-high. Cook lemon zest until sizzling, about 30 seconds. Add broccolini, and cook, stirring, just until warmed through. Transfer to a platter, season with salt, and add lemon juice.

Ⓥ Ⓖ Ⓢ Per serving: 70 calories, 2.33 g fat (0.33 g saturated fat), 0 mg cholesterol, 8.66 g carbohydrates, 4.03 g protein, 1.36 g fiber

Roasted Mixed Cabbages

When cabbage is slow-roasted, the leafy edges become deliciously charred and caramelized. For added variety, you could also toss halved brussels sprouts, chopped turnips, or shallots into the mix. The cabbages would go well with the Celeriac and Apple Mash on page 355, Mashed White Beans and Vegetables on page 331, or braised lentils. **SERVES 6**

- 5 pounds mixed green and red cabbages (from 3 heads), cored and cut into ¾-inch-thick wedges
- 6 sprigs thyme
- 2 tablespoons plus 1½ teaspoons extra-virgin olive oil
  Coarse salt and freshly ground pepper

Preheat oven to 425°F. On 2 rimmed baking sheets, combine cabbages with thyme and olive oil. Season with salt and pepper. Spread evenly and roast, turning every 15 minutes, until tender and slightly charred, about 1 hour 15 minutes. Serve immediately.

Ⓥ Ⓖ Ⓢ Per serving: 165 calories, 6.5 g fat (0.9 g saturated fat), 0 mg cholesterol, 26.23 g carbohydrates, 5.34 g protein, 8.64 g fiber

Roasted Cauliflower with Lemon and Cilantro

Cauliflower is at its tender, nutty best when roasted. Curry powder, cilantro, and lemon juice are added here for extra flavor, but you could swap those out with other components. Try spices such as paprika or cayenne, and then finish with fresh lime juice and chopped fresh herbs such as parsley. **SERVES 4**

1 head cauliflower (about 1 pound), trimmed and cut crosswise into ½-inch-thick slices

2 tablespoons extra-virgin olive oil

1 teaspoon curry powder

Coarse salt and freshly ground pepper

½ lemon, cut into wedges

Fresh cilantro, for garnish

1 Preheat oven to 450°F. On a rimmed baking sheet, drizzle cauliflower with olive oil, sprinkle with curry powder, and season with salt and pepper. Toss to combine and spread in an even layer. Roast until golden brown underneath, about 15 minutes.

2 Flip cauliflower and continue cooking until tender, about 10 minutes more. Remove from oven. Squeeze lemon over cauliflower, garnish with cilantro, and serve.

V G S Per serving: 98 calories, 7 g fat (6 g saturated fat), 0 mg cholesterol, 11 g carbohydrates, 5 g protein, 5 g fiber

Shredded Brussels Sprouts with Pecans and Mustard Seeds

Mustard seeds are often used to season cabbages in German cooking. Toasting the seeds enhances their flavor, so only a small amount of butter and olive oil are needed to sauté the brussels sprouts. Toasted pecans also bring their own bit of buttery flavor as well as a decent amount of protein. This is a Thanksgiving dish that everyone will be grateful for. **SERVES 4**

- 2 containers (10 ounces each) brussels sprouts, ends trimmed
- ½ tablespoon unsalted butter
- 2 teaspoons olive oil
- 1 tablespoon yellow mustard seeds
- 1 to 2 tablespoons fresh lemon juice
- Coarse salt and ground pepper
- ⅓ cup pecans, toasted (see page 363) and coarsely chopped

1 Shred brussels sprouts using the shredding disk of a food processor (or halve sprouts and thinly slice with a chef's knife).

2 In a large nonstick skillet, heat butter and olive oil over medium-high. Add mustard seeds and cook, stirring, until fragrant, about 30 seconds. Add brussels sprouts and cook, tossing occasionally, until tender and beginning to brown, 7 to 9 minutes. Remove from heat, stir in lemon juice, and season with salt and pepper. Serve topped with pecans.

ⓖ Per serving: 169 calories, 12 g fat (2 g saturated fat), 3.76 mg cholesterol, 14 g carbohydrates, 6 g protein, 6 g fiber

Baby Bok Choy with Chile, Garlic, and Ginger

Bok choy's mild taste calls for assertive flavorings, such as the chile, garlic, and fresh ginger used here. Baby bok choy is especially desirable for its small size and tender leaves, but this recipe can also be made with regular bok choy sliced lengthwise into 1½-inch pieces. Serve with steamed rice, vegetable fried rice (see page 86), Asian noodles, or grilled or broiled tofu. **SERVES 4**

2 teaspoons canola or safflower oil

1 red jalapeño chile, thinly sliced (ribs and seeds removed for less heat if desired)

1 garlic clove, thinly sliced

1 piece (about 1 inch) fresh ginger, peeled and thinly sliced

1 pound baby bok choy, halved lengthwise

3 tablespoons water

Coarse salt

1 Heat oil in a large skillet over medium-high. Add jalapeño, garlic, and ginger and cook, stirring, until tender, about 1 minute.

2 Add bok choy and the water. Cover tightly and steam until tender, 7 to 8 minutes. Uncover, and cook until any remaining liquid evaporates. Season with salt and serve.

Ⓥ Ⓖ Ⓢ Per serving: 40 calories, 2.58 g fat (0.2 g saturated fat), 0 mg cholesterol, 3.24 g carbohydrates, 1.9 g protein, 1.18 g fiber

Roasted Sweet Potatoes with Parsley and Walnut Pesto

A drizzle of pesto gives new life to roasted sweet potato wedges—and would also perk up other roasted vegetables, including cauliflower, Brussels sprouts, and carrots. When roasting the potatoes, leave the skins on for greater nutrition (and better texture). High heat muddies the fresh flavors of the parsley and lemon zest in the pesto, so drizzle it over the potatoes just before serving. **SERVES 4**

4 sweet potatoes, scrubbed and cut into 1-inch wedges

¼ cup plus 3 tablespoons extra-virgin olive oil

Coarse salt and freshly ground pepper

2 cups fresh flat-leaf parsley

¼ teaspoon chopped garlic (about 1 small clove)

½ cup walnuts, toasted (see page 363)

Grated zest of 1 lemon

1 tablespoon fresh lemon juice

1 Preheat oven to 425°F. On a rimmed baking sheet, toss sweet potatoes with 1 tablespoon olive oil and season with salt and pepper. Spread in an even layer; roast, turning once, until golden and tender, about 25 minutes. Let cool slightly.

2 Meanwhile, pulse parsley, garlic, walnuts, zest, and lemon juice in a food processor until coarsely chopped. Add remaining ¼ cup plus 2 tablespoons oil in a steady stream and process until combined. Season with salt and pepper.

3 To serve, drizzle 2 tablespoons pesto over sweet potatoes, and serve the rest alongside.

V G Per serving: 431 calories, 33 g fat (4 g saturated fat), 0 mg cholesterol, 31 g carbohydrates, 5 g protein, 6 g fiber

Three Vegetable Slaws

All three of these slaws forgo mayonnaise-based dressings in favor of two lighter options: olive oil and yogurt.

Golden Beet Slaw SERVES 6

- ¼ cup extra-virgin olive oil
- 2 tablespoons red-wine vinegar
- 1 teaspoon finely grated orange zest
- 1 tablespoon fresh orange juice
- Coarse salt and freshly ground pepper
- 1½ pounds golden beets, peeled and cut into matchsticks
- 3 scallions, trimmed and thinly sliced
- ½ cup chopped fresh cilantro leaves

Whisk oil, vinegar, and zest and juice in a bowl. Season with salt and pepper. Add beets, scallions, and cilantro. Toss to combine and serve.

Ⓥ Ⓖ Ⓢ Per serving: 140 calories, 9.56 g fat (1.34 g saturated fat), 0 mg cholesterol, 12.16 g carbohydrates, 2.11 g protein, 3.58 g fiber

Asparagus and Carrot Slaw SERVES 6

- 3 carrots, peeled
- 1½ pounds asparagus, tough ends trimmed
- ⅓ cup fresh mint leaves
- ⅓ cup thinly sliced red onion
- 2 tablespoons extra-virgin olive oil
- 1 tablespoon fresh lemon juice
- Coarse salt

Grate carrots and asparagus on the large holes of a box grater. Toss with mint, onion, oil, and juice in a bowl. Season with salt and serve.

Ⓥ Ⓖ Ⓢ Per serving: 89 calories, 4.9 g fat (0.72 g saturated fat), 0 mg cholesterol, 8.32 g carbohydrates, 2.91 g protein, 3.42 g fiber

Cabbage and Green Apple Slaw SERVES 6

- ½ cup plain low-fat yogurt
- 1 fresh red chile, seeded and finely chopped
- 1 tablespoon apple cider vinegar
- 1 tablespoon minced peeled fresh ginger
- 1 teaspoon toasted black mustard seeds (see page 363)
- ½ teaspoon toasted cumin seeds (see page 363)
- Coarse salt
- 3 cups shredded cabbage
- 2 Granny Smith apples, cut into matchsticks

Whisk yogurt, chile, vinegar, ginger, and both seeds in a bowl. Season with salt. Stir in cabbage and apples and serve.

Ⓖ Per serving: 53 calories, 0.7 g fat (0.24 g saturated fat), 0 mg cholesterol, 11.11 g carbohydrates, 1.94 g protein, 2.14 g fiber

Sauté-Steamed Swiss Chard

Commit this cooking method to memory for using with all your leafy greens. The cooking time will vary according to how young and small the greens are, so taste as you cook to judge the degree of doneness. Try red, green, or rainbow chard or substitutes like beet greens, bok choy, mizuna (a variety of Japanese mustard green with sawtooth leaves), and spinach. The greens would be delicious over polenta or with scrambled eggs for breakfast. **SERVES 4**

1½ pounds Swiss chard, tough stem ends trimmed

1 tablespoon plus 1½ teaspoons olive oil

3 garlic cloves, pressed or minced

½ cup water

Coarse salt and freshly ground pepper

1 lemon, cut into wedges

1 Wash Swiss chard well and drain, leaving water clinging to leaves. With a chef's knife or your hands, separate leaves from stems. Cut stems crosswise into ½-inch pieces. Stack leaves, roll them, and cut crosswise into ½-inch ribbons.

2 In a large heavy pot or Dutch oven, heat olive oil over medium. Add garlic and cook, stirring, until golden, about 1 minute. Stir in chard stems; reduce heat to medium-low, cover, and cook, stirring occasionally until stems have softened, 3 to 5 minutes.

3 Add damp chard leaves and the water. Cover and cook, stirring occasionally, until the greens are completely wilted and tender, 3 to 6 minutes. Season with salt and pepper. Serve immediately on a platter or in a bowl, with lemon wedges on the side.

V G S Per serving: 82 calories, 5 g fat (1 g saturated fat), 0 mg cholesterol, 8 g carbohydrates, 3 g protein, 3 g fiber

Quinoa and Green Bean Salad

More vegetables, fewer grains—that's what gives this salad a fresh personality, along with the extra flavor provided by a full cup of parsley. Here, quinoa plays a supporting role to blanched green beans, providing a bit of protein to the dish. **SERVES 8**

½ cup plus 1 tablespoon extra-virgin olive oil

1 small onion, minced

2 garlic cloves, minced

Coarse salt and freshly ground pepper

1 cup quinoa, rinsed and drained

1¾ cups water

1 pound green beans, trimmed

1 cup fresh flat-leaf parsley leaves

3 tablespoons red-wine vinegar

1. Heat 1 tablespoon olive oil in a medium saucepan over medium-high. Add onion and garlic and season with salt and pepper. Cook, stirring, until onion is translucent, about 3 minutes. Stir in quinoa and cook, stirring, for 1 minute. Add the water and bring to a boil. Reduce to a simmer and cook, covered, until quinoa is tender and water is absorbed, about 15 minutes. Remove from heat. Let stand 10 minutes; fluff with fork. Let cool completely.

2. Meanwhile, cook beans in a pot of boiling salted water until crisp-tender and bright green, about 4 minutes. Drain and rinse in cold water to stop the cooking and cool completely.

3. Combine quinoa mixture, green beans, and parsley in a large bowl. Toss with remaining ½ cup oil and the vinegar; season with salt and pepper, and serve.

Ⓥ Ⓖ Ⓢ Per serving: 143 calories, 7 g fat (1 g saturated fat), 0 mg cholesterol, 16 g carbohydrates, 3 g protein, 2.68 g fiber

Roasted Brussels Sprouts and Grapes with Walnuts

Here's another great Thanksgiving side dish that uses brussels sprouts in a surprising way, this time roasted alongside grapes and topped with walnuts (or pecans, if you prefer). Balsamic vinegar is drizzled over the sprouts after roasting to incorporate the flavorful bits from the bottom of the baking sheet. Choose sprouts that are about an inch in diameter; larger sprouts can be bitter. **SERVES 8**

1½ pounds brussels sprouts (about 8 cups), halved or quartered if large

1½ pounds red seedless grapes (about 4 cups)

2 tablespoons extra-virgin olive oil

¼ cup fresh thyme leaves

Coarse salt and freshly ground pepper

2 teaspoons balsamic vinegar

½ cup walnuts, toasted (see page 363) and coarsely chopped

1 Preheat oven to 450°F. On 2 rimmed baking sheets, toss brussels sprouts and grapes with olive oil and thyme, dividing evenly. Season with salt and pepper. Roast until tender and browned, tossing occasionally, about 20 minutes.

2 Drizzle each sheet with 1 teaspoon vinegar and scrape up any caramelized bits with a wooden spoon. Add walnuts; toss to combine, and serve.

V G Per serving: 169 calories, 8 g fat (1 g saturated fat), 0 mg cholesterol, 24 g carbohydrates, 4 g protein, 4 g fiber

VERSATILE VEGETARIAN:
MASHES AND PUREES

Practically any vegetable can be mashed or pureed to produce a variety of textures—from velvety smooth to fluffy and light, or even coarse and rustic (think "smashes"). The potatoes and root vegetables here make especially delicious versions, but peas, fennel, broccoli, cauliflower, and asparagus are other fine options. First cook the vegetables until tender, then mash or puree, adding a small amount of oil or butter and herbs or spices. For such minimal effort, you'll be rewarded with rich-tasting side dishes that have broad appeal.

COOK VEGETABLES

DRAIN

MASH

SMASHED PARSNIPS AND POTATOES WITH THYME SERVES 4

¼ cup extra-virgin olive oil, plus more for drizzling

½ pound parsnips, peeled and cut into ½-inch pieces

Coarse salt and freshly ground pepper

1½ pounds baby Yukon Gold potatoes, quartered

1 tablespoon plus 1½ teaspoons fresh thyme leaves

1. Heat 1 tablespoon olive oil in a medium saucepan over medium. Cook parsnips with ¼ teaspoon salt, stirring occasionally, 5 minutes. Add potatoes, 1½ teaspoons salt, and enough water to cover by 1 inch. Bring to a boil, then reduce heat and simmer until parsnips and potatoes are very tender but still hold their shape, 12 to 14 minutes. Drain.

2. Return empty saucepan to high heat, allowing any remaining water to evaporate. Add remaining 3 tablespoons oil and the thyme. Cook, stirring, until thyme starts to sizzle, about 1 minute.

3. Add parsnips and potatoes, and smash with a potato masher or the back of a wooden spoon until combined but still chunky. Season with salt and pepper. Drizzle with more oil and serve immediately.

V G S Per serving: 287 calories, 14.36 g fat (2.05 g saturated fat), 0 mg cholesterol, 37.14 g carbohydrates, 3.59 g protein, 6.99 g fiber

Roasted-Beet-and-Tomato Puree with Orange SERVES 6

- 1 pound ripe plum tomatoes, quartered and seeded
- 1 teaspoon chopped fresh thyme
- 3 tablespoons extra-virgin olive oil
  Coarse salt
- 2½ pounds red beets, scrubbed and trimmed
- 1 tablespoon plus 1 teaspoon orange juice

Preheat oven to 375°F. Toss tomatoes with thyme and 1 tablespoon oil on a rimmed baking sheet; season with salt. Spread in a single layer on half the sheet. Toss beets with remaining oil, and season with salt. Wrap beets in parchment and then foil, and place on other half of sheet. Roast until tomatoes are softened and beets are tender, 45 to 50 minutes. Let cool slightly, then peel beets and coarsely chop. Working in two batches, puree tomatoes and beets in a food processor. Transfer to a bowl. Stir in orange juice, season with salt, and serve.

V G Per serving: 160 calories, 7.48 g fat (1.05 g saturated fat), 0 mg cholesterol, 21.42 g carbohydrates, 3.74 g protein, 6.22 g fiber

Mashed Carrots with Honey and Chili Powder SERVES 4

- 1½ pounds carrots, peeled, halved lengthwise if large, and cut into 1-inch pieces
- 1 tablespoon unsalted butter
- 2 teaspoons honey
- ½ teaspoon chili powder
  Coarse salt and freshly ground pepper

Set a steamer basket in a saucepan filled with 2 inches simmering water. Add carrots; cover and steam until very tender, 25 minutes. Transfer to a bowl and mash. Stir in butter, honey, and chili powder; season with salt and pepper, and serve.

G Per serving: 106 calories, 3.3 g fat (1.9 g saturated fat), 7.53 mg cholesterol, 19.3 g carbohydrates, 1.7 g protein, 4.9 g fiber

Celeriac and Apple Mash SERVES 6

- 1¾ cups vegetable stock, preferably homemade (see page 364)
- 1 cup water
- 1 pound celeriac, peeled and cut into 1-inch pieces
- 1 pound Yukon Gold potatoes, peeled and cut into 1-inch pieces
- 1 Granny Smith apple, peeled, cored, and cut into 1-inch pieces
- 1 shallot, coarsely chopped
- 1 bay leaf
  Coarse salt
- 2 tablespoons unsalted butter
- ¾ ounce blue cheese (about 2 tablespoons), plus more for serving

In a large pot, combine vegetable stock, the water, celeriac, potatoes, apple, shallot, and bay leaf. Bring to a boil, then add 1 teaspoon salt. Cook until vegetables are tender, about 10 minutes. Drain in a sieve, reserving liquid; discard bay leaf. Return celeriac, potatoes, apple, and shallot to pot, and add ¾ cup reserved cooking liquid. Coarsely mash with a potato masher. Using a fork, mash together butter and blue cheese in a small bowl. Stir into celeriac mixture; season with salt. Spoon into a warm bowl, and crumble more blue cheese over the top.

G Per serving: 160 calories, 5.15 g fat (3.15 g saturated fat), 12.69 mg cholesterol, 26.11 g carbohydrates, 3.86 g protein, 3.91 g fiber

the vegetarian pantry

BEANS AND OTHER LEGUMES

Though small in size and plain in appearance, legumes—which include beans and lentils (as well as chickpeas, soybeans, peas, green beans, and peanuts)—are indispensable in the vegetarian kitchen. They contribute a savory taste and dense, substantial texture to all sorts of dishes as well as plenty of protein and fiber. When combined with whole grains, they also create a complete protein (see page 11).

• Pair beans with rice, or use them in chilis and other stews, as a filling for enchiladas or tacos, or in composed salads. They can also be mashed to make dips, incorporated into veggie burgers, or served as a main course or side dish on their own. Lentils, which cook more quickly than other beans, are perfect for soups and salads.

• Canned beans are convenient for quick meals, but dried varieties are more economical and don't have added sodium. Store dried beans in airtight containers up to a year. Before cooking, pick through them to remove any stones or other debris, then soak and cook as described on page 365. If using canned beans, drain and rinse before cooking or eating.

WHOLE GRAINS AND QUINOA

High in complex carbohydrates and fiber, whole grains are a great source of energy. Wheat berries, barley, rice, farro, bulgur, and millet are all examples of whole grains. Quinoa is actually the seed of a plant related to spinach and not technically a grain; as a so-called complete protein, quinoa is one of the only plant-based sources of all nine essential amino acids (nutritional building blocks).

• One of the easiest ways to enjoy whole grains is to toss them with vegetables or herbs in a salad (as in the recipes on pages 231 and 232); you can also use them in risottos, pilafs, soups, or fillings for stuffed vegetables. See page 371 for cooking instructions for the most widely available grains.

• Since cooked grains are so versatile, make more than you need; toss extra grains with a little olive oil, season with salt and pepper, and keep in the refrigerator up to 5 days.

• Most grains can be purchased in packages or from bulk bins at health-food stores and well-stocked supermarkets; they are best stored in airtight glass jars or canisters in a cool, dry place. To discourage pantry pests, place a bay leaf or dried chile pepper in the container. Grains will generally keep six months to one year.

PASTA

Pasta is a favorite option for vegetarian cooking, and with good reason: it's the perfect partner for nearly any vegetable or sauce, it cooks quickly, and it's a time-tested crowd-pleaser.

• Pasta can be tossed with nothing other than olive oil and herbs to make a delicious meal. Combine pasta with beans and vegetables in a robust salad. Baked pastas are classic comfort foods; for a more nutritionally balanced meal, switch up the proportions a little and allow the vegetables to take the lead. The key to all great pasta is generously salting the cooking water so that it is "salty like the sea."

• Choose whole-grain versions, such as those made from spelt, whole wheat, or farro, when you can: they contain more fiber and have distinctive flavors. Gluten-free varieties made from brown rice, lentils, quinoa, or corn are increasingly available. Soba, or buckwheat, noodles are the traditional choice for Japanese noodle dishes; they also provide more protein than many other varieties (and those labeled 100% buckwheat are also gluten-free). Pastas can be stored in their original packaging until opened, then transferred to airtight containers. They are best used within one year of purchase.

EGGS

Although some vegetarians don't eat eggs, those who do benefit from their high protein content and culinary versatility.

• Top salads or sandwiches with poached eggs, add scrambled eggs to fried rice, or use them to make omelets or frittatas. Hard-boiled eggs keep for about a week; boil a few on Sunday and then use them throughout the week in sandwiches and salads or as a snack.

• The best place to buy ethically farmed eggs is at farmer's markets, where you can talk to farmers about their practices. If you buy eggs at the grocery store, look for terms such as "cage free" or "pasture raised," but be mindful that these labels aren't regulated by the USDA. The USDA does regulate the term "organic," which means the birds are raised without antibiotics, given organic feed, and provided some access to the outdoors.

• Keep eggs in their original carton in the body of the refrigerator, not in the door (otherwise the eggs are jostled and subjected to temperature changes each time the door opens). Eggs should keep for several weeks. Here's an easy way to test for freshness: Gently drop an egg in a glass of water. If it floats to the top it may be spoiled; if it sinks to the bottom or hovers in the middle, it's still safe to eat.

NUTS AND SEEDS

A variety of nuts and seeds, such as almonds, walnuts, pine nuts, and sunflower seeds, can be used to add protein and crunch to many meatless dishes.

• Sprinkle nuts onto salads, pastas, and vegetable sides, blend them into pestos, or enjoy them as an energy-boosting snack.

• Buy nuts from a source with high turnover to avoid any that are stale or rancid. You can store them in the pantry, but they will last longer—up to six months—in the freezer.

TOFU, TEMPEH, AND SEITAN

Don't think of tofu, tempeh, and seitan as "meat substitutes"—think of them instead as distinct ingredients with their own tastes and virtues. Used thoughtfully, they add protein, flavor, and substance.

• Tofu (pressed cakes of soybean curd) may be familiar, even to meat eaters, as a staple of Asian cuisines, and you'll commonly find it in stir-fries, noodle soups, and curries. It comes in silken, soft, firm, and extra-firm varieties: silken tofu is ideal for pureeing into sauces, smoothies, or even desserts; soft works well in soups; and firm or extra-firm is best for frying or grilling (press it first to remove excess moisture; see instructions on page 363). Packages of water-packed tofu come with a sell-by date; any unused portion can be drained, covered with fresh water, and refrigerated in an airtight container up to one week. Unopened vacuum-packed (shelf-stable) tofu will keep at room temperature up to eight months.

• Like tofu, tempeh is made from soy; but unlike tofu, it is made from the whole beans, and has a denser texture and stronger flavor. Cut or crumble it into small pieces and add it to stir-fries instead of tofu, or in place of ground beef in chili or hash (see page 85). Store tempeh in an airtight container in the refrigerator up to a week, or in the freezer up to 3 months.

• Seitan, popular in Buddhist and macrobiotic diets, is made from wheat gluten, not soy. It is known for its dense, meaty texture and flavor; cut it into slices and use it for sandwiches, kebabs, and casseroles (see a recipe for homemade seitan on page 366). Refrigerate seitan in its broth up to one week, or freeze in individual portions, wrapped in parchment, up to one month.

CHEESE

Cheese can often enhance vegetable-based dishes by contributing richness and flavor, even when used in small amounts. A cheese board is a lovely addition when entertaining or when eating a selection of small plates, and a bite of cheese eaten with fruit, nuts, or pickles also makes a healthy snack.

• When cooking, new combinations or previously unfamiliar cheeses can refresh old favorites such as pizzas, burgers, and pastas; a bit of cheese crumbled over salads and vegetable side dishes makes them more filling and satisfying to eat.

• Keep cheeses in the cheese compartment of the refrigerator, wrapped in cheesecloth, parchment or wax paper, or its original packaging. Do not completely enclose cheese in plastic wrap, which will prevent it from "breathing;" if you choose to wrap it in plastic, leave the rind exposed. Cheese will generally keep for three to four weeks, while some hard cheeses (such as aged Parmigiano-Reggiano) last months, and some softer ones (such as feta) only days. For fresh or higher-end cheeses, it's best to buy only the amount that you will need.

OILS AND VINEGARS

The classic pair of oil and vinegar is essential for cooking and for dressing salads; choosing a few varieties of each allows for maximum versatility. At the very least, you'll want one neutral-tasting vegetable oil for high-heat cooking and good-quality extra-virgin olive oil for dressings.

• Extra-virgin olive oil is delicious in vinaigrettes and drizzled onto finished dishes; it's also high in monounsaturated fat, which can lower cholesterol and blood pressure. Extra-virgin olive oil is not recommended for cooking at high temperatures, though, as it has a low smoke point. Other flavorful oils, such as walnut, hazelnut, almond, and toasted sesame oil, can be used in the same manner as extra-virgin olive oil.

• Safflower, canola, and grapeseed oils are neutral tasting and have a high smoke point, which means they can withstand high temperatures without burning or smoking. Use them for sautéing, frying, or stir-frying.

• Keep a variety of vinegars on hand for cooking and for dressing salads. Balsamic, cider, white or red wine, rice wine, and sherry are the most frequently used.

• Store most oils and vinegars in their original bottles in a cool, dark place—oils for up to six months and vinegars up to one year. Nut oils should be refrigerated and used within three to six months.

SPICES AND HERBS

The spices and herbs you choose will depend on personal preference, but it also helps to stock a well-rounded assortment.

• A "starter kit" of spices might include cinnamon, nutmeg, cumin, chili powder or cayenne, and red pepper flakes, plus whole black peppercorns for grinding; customize your pantry with additions such as smoked paprika, curry powder, garam masala, coriander, cardamom, and turmeric. Keep spices in airtight containers away from light and heat (do not store them above the stovetop). Most spices will lose their potency after about a year; mark the date of purchase on each bottle so you'll know when it's time to replace.

• Fresh herbs are another great way to boost flavor, both in cooking and as garnishes. Fresh herbs are preferred over dried for their pure, bright flavors. Rinse and dry herbs carefully before using, without crushing the leaves. Store them in the refrigerator in a resealable plastic bag between layers of barely damp paper towels for up to one week. Dried herbs are more potent than fresh, so if you substitute them in a recipe, decrease the quantity to one-quarter the amount. Store dried herbs as you would ground spices, in a cool, dark place.

MARINATED ROASTED
RED PEPPERS

QUICK PICKLES

COOKED LENTILS

TAPENADE

SLOW-ROASTED TOMATOES

CARAMELIZED ONIONS

ROASTED GARLIC

ALL-PURPOSE
VINAIGRETTE

favorite flavor boosters

Putting together a meal is much easier when you have a handful of flavor-packed components at the ready. The following ones keep well in the refrigerator and can be incorporated into a range of dishes such as bruschetta, pizzas, soups and stews, salads (including grain-based versions), sandwiches and vegetable burgers, pastas, and omelets and frittatas.

Marinated Roasted Red Peppers   MAKES 2 CUPS

Slice 3 roasted **RED PEPPERS** (see page 364) into 1-inch-wide strips. Toss with ½ cup **EXTRA-VIRGIN OLIVE OIL**, 3 tablespoons **BALSAMIC VINEGAR**, and 1 very thinly sliced **GARLIC** clove. Season with coarse **SALT** and freshly ground **PEPPER**. Refrigerate in an airtight container up to 1 week. Bring to room temperature before using.

Quick Pickles   MAKES 2½ QUARTS

Use this master recipe to pickle cucumber or other sliced vegetables such as carrots, beets, red onions, or trimmed green beans. In a bowl, toss 2 pounds **KIRBY CUCUMBERS**, sliced diagonally ¼ inch thick; 3 small **ONIONS** (optional), cut into ½-inch wedges; and 3 tablespoons coarse **SALT**. Cover; refrigerate 2 hours. In a saucepan over medium heat, cook 2 cups **CIDER VINEGAR**, 1¾ cups packed **LIGHT-BROWN SUGAR**, 1 tablespoon **MUSTARD SEEDS**, and ¾ teaspoon **CELERY SEEDS**, stirring to dissolve sugar. Rinse and drain cucumber mixture. Pour vinegar mixture over; let cool. Refrigerate in an airtight container up to 3 weeks.

Tapenade   MAKES 1¼ CUPS

Pulse 2 cups pitted **BLACK OLIVES**, such as kalamata, ½ cup fresh flat-leaf **PARSLEY** leaves; and 1 **GARLIC** clove in a food processor until coarsely chopped. Stir in 2 tablespoons **EXTRA-VIRGIN OLIVE OIL**. Refrigerate in an airtight container up to 2 weeks.

Slow-Roasted Tomatoes   MAKES 24 HALVES

Preheat oven to 325°F. Halve 12 **PLUM TOMATOES** (about 4 pounds total) lengthwise. Arrange tomatoes, cut side up, in a single layer on two rimmed baking sheets. Dividing evenly, drizzle with ¼ cup **EXTRA-VIRGIN OLIVE OIL** and sprinkle with 4 teaspoons chopped fresh **THYME** and coarse **SALT** and freshly ground **PEPPER** to taste. Roast until softened, about 90 minutes. Let cool completely. Refrigerate in an airtight container up to 5 days.

Roasted Garlic   MAKES 2 CUPS

Preheat oven to 400°F. Using a serrated knife, slice off the top quarter of 6 to 8 **GARLIC** heads (about 1 pound total). Arrange cut side up in a baking dish. Season with coarse **SALT** and freshly ground **PEPPER**. Drizzle evenly with ½ cup **EXTRA-VIRGIN OLIVE OIL**. Cover dish tightly with parchment, then foil; roast until cloves are golden and soft, about 1 hour. Let stand just until cool enough to handle, then squeeze out cloves. Transfer garlic and oil to an airtight container, and refrigerate up to 2 weeks.

All-Purpose Vinaigrette MAKES 1 CUP

In a small bowl, whisk ¼ cup **WHITE-WINE VINEGAR** (or substitute red-wine, sherry, or balsamic vinegar or fresh lemon juice) and 1 tablespoon **DIJON MUSTARD**; season with coarse **SALT** and freshly ground **PEPPER**. If desired, add 1 teaspoon minced **GARLIC**, 3 chopped **SCALLIONS**, or 2 tablespoons chopped fresh **HERBS**. Slowly add ¾ cup **EXTRA-VIRGIN OLIVE OIL**, whisking until emulsified. (Alternatively, shake the ingredients in a jar.) Refrigerate in an airtight container up to 2 weeks; whisk (or shake) before using.

Caramelized Onions MAKES 2 CUPS

In a large heavy skillet, heat ¼ cup **OLIVE OIL** over medium-high. Add 2½ pounds **ONIONS**, peeled, halved lengthwise, and sliced ¼ inch thick; sprinkle with 1 teaspoon **SUGAR**. Cook, stirring occasionally, until translucent, about 15 minutes. Reduce heat to medium and continue cooking, stirring frequently, until deep golden brown, 30 to 45 minutes more. (If onions begin to darken too quickly, stir in a little water. Adjust heat if onions are cooking too quickly or too slowly.) Add 1 to 2 tablespoons water and scrape to combine brown bits from bottom of pan. Remove from heat; season with coarse **SALT**. Let cool completely. Refrigerate in an airtight container up to 2 weeks.

Seasoned Lentils MAKES 1¼ CUPS

In a medium saucepan, bring ½ cup dried green **LENTILS** (picked over and rinsed), 2 thinly sliced **GARLIC** cloves, and water to cover by 2 inches to a boil over high. Reduce heat and simmer until the lentils are tender, about 25 minutes. Season with coarse **SALT** and freshly ground **PEPPER** and let cool completely; drain. Refrigerate lentils in an airtight container up to 5 days.

FLAVOR BOOSTERS FROM THE PANTRY

The standout ingredients below are so much more than condiments: reach for one of these items to instantly invigorate your cooking. Chiles and chili sauces add heat, for example; tomato paste, soy sauce, and nut butters contribute their own flavors and textures.

- Asian chile sauce, such as Sriracha or sambal oelek

- assorted mustards

- chile oil

- chipotles in adobo or other canned chiles

- curry pastes

- hot-pepper sauce, such as Tabasco

- nut butters, such as peanut, almond, or cashew

- preserves and chutneys

- soy sauce or tamari

- salt-packed or brined capers

- tahini (sesame seed paste)

- tomato paste

basics

SOFT-COOKING EGGS

Place (room-temperature) eggs in a small saucepan, and add enough cold water to cover by 1 inch. Bring to a boil. Cook for 3 minutes. Remove eggs from saucepan.

HARD-COOKING EGGS

Place eggs in a deep saucepan and cover with cold water by 1 inch. Bring to a boil over high heat, then immediately remove from heat, cover, and let stand 13 minutes. Use a slotted spoon to transfer eggs to an ice-water bath to stop the cooking. Unpeeled eggs can be refrigerated up to 1 week.

POACHING EGGS

Fill a large deep saucepan with 2 inches of water and bring to a boil. Reduce heat to medium. When the water is barely simmering, break egg into a small heatproof cup or bowl. Placing lip of cup in the water, gently tip the cup to slide egg carefully into the pan. Repeat with more eggs, if desired. Cook until whites are just set but yolks are still soft (they should still move around inside), 2 to 3 minutes. Lift out eggs with a slotted spoon or small mesh sieve and briefly rest on paper towels to drain.

PRESSING TOFU

When pressed to remove excess water, tofu becomes denser and firmer, holds its shape, and browns better when cooked. Lay cut tofu flat on a baking sheet lined with a double layer of paper towels. Place two more clean towels on top and add another baking sheet. Weight with a heavy skillet or canned goods; let sit 20 to 30 minutes.

TOASTING NUTS AND SEEDS

- To toast nuts such as almonds, walnuts, or pecans, spread them on a rimmed baking sheet and cook in a 350°F oven until fragrant, tossing once or twice, about 10 minutes. (Start checking after 6 minutes if toasting sliced or chopped nuts.)

- Toast pine nuts at 350°F for 5 to 7 minutes, and pepitas (pumpkin seeds) or sunflower seeds at 300°F for about 12 minutes, or until lightly browned.

- Toast hazelnuts in a 375°F oven until skins split, 10 to 12 minutes; when cool enough to handle, rub warm nuts in a clean kitchen towel to remove skins.

- Toast sesame seeds in a small skillet over medium heat, shaking the pan occasionally, until golden, 2 to 3 minutes (be careful not to let them burn). Transfer to a plate to cool.

MAKING BREAD CRUMBS

Trim off crusts from a loaf of bread (preferably whole-wheat or whole-grain), and tear the bread into large pieces. Pulse in a food processor to form coarse or fine crumbs, as desired. (For dried bread crumbs, toast the crumbs on a rimmed baking sheet in a 250°F oven 12 to 15 minutes.) Leftover bread crumbs can be frozen, in an airtight container, for 3 months.

PREPARING COUSCOUS

Toss couscous with a small amount of olive oil, coating evenly, in a heatproof bowl. Pour boiling water over couscous (use an equal amount of water and couscous). Cover and let stand until couscous has absorbed the water, about 5 minutes. Fluff with a fork.

BLANCHING AND PEELING TOMATOES

Slice an X into the bottom of each tomato with a paring knife. Blanch in a pot of boiling water for about 10 seconds. Use a slotted spoon to remove tomatoes from pot, and plunge into an ice-water bath until cool enough to handle. Starting at the X, use a paring knife to remove the skin.

ROASTING PEPPERS OR CHILES

Roast peppers or chiles (such as poblanos) over a gas flame, turning with tongs, until charred all over. Transfer to a bowl, cover with a large plate, and let stand until cool enough to handle. Scrape skins off with a paring knife. (Do not run roasted peppers under water.) Remove and discard stems, ribs, and seeds.

PREPARING ARTICHOKES

To trim artichokes: Using a serrated knife, cut off top quarter of the artichoke. Use kitchen shears to trim sharp tips of artichoke leaves. Remove small leaves from bottom of artichoke, and trim stem if necessary. To prepare hearts: Cut off top of artichoke and pluck small leaves from trimmed bottom. Use a paring knife to remove remaining leaves and trim dark green parts from outside of stem. Using a melon baller or small spoon, remove the fuzzy purple choke. If not using immediately, add artichoke heart to a bowl of acidulated water (squeeze juice of half a lemon into a bowl of water) to prevent discoloration.

TESTING HEAT FOR CHARCOAL GRILLS

To gauge the heat of a charcoal grill, hold your hand about 5 inches above the grate: you should only be able to hold your hand there 2 to 3 full seconds for high heat; 3 to 4 seconds for medium-high; and 4 to 5 seconds for medium.

basic recipes

VEGETABLE STOCK

This stock freezes well, so you may want to make a couple of batches (just double the recipe) to use in all your vegetarian cooking. To crush peppercorns, press with the bottom of a small skillet; or crush with the side of a large knife on a cutting board.

2 leeks, white and pale-green parts only, cut into 1-inch rounds, washed well and drained

2 carrots, peeled and cut into 1-inch rounds

1 small onion, cut into 1-inch pieces

3 garlic cloves

8 cups water

5 sprigs flat-leaf parsley

2 sprigs thyme

1 dried bay leaf

2 teaspoons whole black peppercorns, crushed

1 Combine leeks, carrots, onion, and garlic in a medium saucepan. Cover; cook over medium heat, stirring occasionally, for 10 minutes.

2 Add the water, herbs, and peppercorns. Bring to a boil. Reduce heat. Simmer, uncovered, 30 minutes. Pour through a cheesecloth-lined strainer; discard solids. Once cool, stock can be refrigerated for up to 2 days or frozen for up to 3 months.

MAKES 6 CUPS

🅥 🅖 🅢 Per serving (1½ cups): 20 calories, 0 g fat, 0 mg cholesterol, 11 g carbohydrates, 1 g protein, 0 g fiber

A PERFECT POT OF BEANS

This recipe works for any kind of dried bean. The cooking time, however, will depend on the variety and age of the beans, so check the consistency frequently as they cook, starting after thirty to forty-five minutes. The beans need to soak at least eight hours before cooking, so plan accordingly. Or, try this quick-soaking method: place beans in a large saucepan, cover with cold water, and bring to a rapid boil. Turn off the heat and allow beans to soak, covered, for 1 hour. Drain and rinse before cooking. When substituting dried beans for canned, or vice versa, use this rule of thumb: One 15.5-ounce can equals approximately 1½ cups cooked beans.

- 1 pound dried beans, such as chickpeas, kidney, cannellini, navy, black, or pinto, picked over and rinsed
- 2 tablespoons extra-virgin olive oil
- 1 onion, chopped
- 3 garlic cloves, chopped
- 1 fresh chile, such as jalapeño or serrano, chopped (optional)
  Coarse salt

1 Place beans in a large bowl or pot. (Beans can expand to twice their size, so choose a bowl big enough to accommodate them.) Add water to cover generously and refrigerate at least 8 and up to 24 hours. Drain and rinse before cooking.

2 Heat olive oil in a large pot over medium. Add onion, garlic, and chile (if using), and season with salt. Cook, stirring frequently, until onion is soft, about 5 minutes.

3 Add beans, 8 cups water, and 1½ teaspoons salt. Bring to a boil. Reduce heat and simmer, partially covered and adding water as needed to keep beans submerged, until beans are tender all the way through, 35 minutes to 2 hours. (Take a few out to test for doneness; beans should mash easily with a fork.) If not using right away, let beans cool in the cooking liquid. Refrigerate in an airtight container up to 5 days or freeze up to 3 months.

MAKES 6 CUPS

Ⓥ Ⓖ Ⓢ Per serving (1 cup): 304 calories, 4.71 g fat (0.66 g saturated fat), 0 mg cholesterol, 48.54 g carbohydrates, 15.03 g protein, 6.71 g fiber

MARINATED TOFU

- 1 teaspoon Dijon mustard
- 1 tablespoon toasted-sesame oil
- 1 garlic clove, minced
- 2 to 3 tablespoons low-sodium soy sauce, or to taste
- 14 ounces (1 package) extra-firm tofu, drained and pressed (see page 363)
- 1 tablespoon canola or safflower oil

1 In a large shallow dish, combine mustard, sesame oil, garlic, and soy sauce. Place tofu in dish, and turn once to coat evenly with marinade. Let marinate at least 20 minutes at room temperature.

2 Heat canola oil in a large cast-iron pan over medium-high. Add tofu; cook until golden and crisp, about 1 to 2 minutes per side. Serve immediately.

SERVES 4

Ⓥ Per serving: 155 calories, 12 g fat (0.75 g saturated fat), 0 mg cholesterol, 3.61 g carbohydrates, 9.3 g protein, 1.35 g fiber

ALL-PURPOSE SEITAN

Bragg Liquid Aminos is a protein-rich liquid derived from soybeans that has an intensely savory flavor similar to that of soy sauce (which can be substituted). Vital wheat gluten flour has a higher proportion of protein (called gluten) than other types of flour and is used for bread baking as well as for making seitan. You can find both of these items, as well as nutritional yeast seasoning, at natural-foods stores and from online retailers.

FOR THE DOUGH

- 2½ cups vital wheat gluten flour
- ¼ cup garbanzo bean flour
- ¼ cup nutritional yeast seasoning
- 1 teaspoon garlic powder
- 1 teaspoon ground ginger
- ¼ teaspoon coarse salt
- ¼ teaspoon freshly ground pepper
- ¾ cup cold vegetable stock, preferably homemade (see page 364)
- ¾ cup cold water
- ¼ cup Bragg Liquid Aminos or low-sodium soy sauce
- 2 tablespoons extra-virgin olive oil

FOR THE STOCK

- 4 cups vegetable stock, preferably homemade (see page 364)
- 4 cups water
- ¼ cup Bragg Liquid Aminos or low-sodium soy sauce
- 2 tablespoons fresh lemon juice

1. Make the dough: combine dry ingredients in a bowl and wet ingredients in another bowl. Add wet ingredients to the dry, mixing with a fork until blended completely. Transfer dough to a clean surface and knead by hand 10 times. Let rest 3 minutes. Knead 10 to 15 times more; let rest 15 minutes.

2. Meanwhile, make the stock: bring vegetable stock, the water, Bragg Liquid Aminos, and lemon juice to a boil in a pot. Reduce to a simmer and cover pot.

3. Roll dough into a thick log (about 3 inches wide by 8 inches long). Cut crosswise into eight ½-inch-thick pieces and flatten to about ¼-inch thickness. Add dough to stock, cover, and simmer until the middle of each disk is as firm as the edges, 1 to 1½ hours. (Add just enough water to keep dough submerged during cooking. Be sure the stock does not boil.) Remove from heat and let cool, uncovered, in cooking liquid. Once cool, refrigerate in liquid for up to 1 week; or wrap each disk in parchment and freeze in a resealable plastic bag up to 1 month.

MAKES ABOUT 2 POUNDS

V Per serving (8 ounces): 197 calories, 4 g fat (1 g saturated fat), 0 mg cholesterol, 9 g carbohydrates, 31 g protein, 1 g fiber

BASIC POLENTA

- 1 teaspoon coarse salt
- 1 dried bay leaf
- 1 cup coarse-ground polenta (cornmeal)
  Freshly ground pepper
- 1 tablespoon extra-virgin olive oil or unsalted butter, for serving (optional)
  Shaved Parmigiano-Reggiano, for serving (optional)

1. Bring 3 cups cold water, the salt, and bay leaf to a boil in a Dutch oven or a heavy stockpot. Bring 2 cups water to a simmer in a small saucepan over medium heat.

2. Add the polenta to large pot in handfuls, whisking constantly until combined. Reduce heat so that only a couple of large bubbles appear at a time on the surface.

3. Whisk two ladlefuls of simmering water from small pan into polenta, and cook, stirring frequently with a wooden spoon, until water has been absorbed, about 5 minutes. Continue to add two ladlefuls of water every 5 minutes, stirring often and waiting for it to be absorbed before adding more, until polenta is creamy and just pulls away from sides of pot, about 45 minutes. (Adjust heat as needed during cooking.)

4. If not serving immediately, reduce heat to lowest setting, cover pot, and keep warm up

to 1 hour. Remove bay leaf and season with pepper before serving. When ready to serve, stir in olive oil or butter, and serve with a damp spoon. Top each serving with shaved Parmigiano-Reggiano.

5 For firm polenta, omit olive oil and Parmigiano-Reggiano. Pour polenta into a slightly damp 8-inch square baking dish. Let stand until no longer steaming, about 10 minutes. Refrigerate, uncovered, until cold and firm, about 1½ hours. Cover with plastic wrap. Refrigerate until ready to serve, up to 2 days.

MAKES 3½ CUPS

V G Per serving (without butter and Parmesan; for 4 servings): 130 calories, 0.5 g fat (0 g saturated fat), 0 mg cholesterol, 27 g carbohydrates, 3 g protein, 2 g fiber

BÉCHAMEL SAUCE

6 cups low-fat milk

6 tablespoons (¾ stick) unsalted butter, cut into pieces

¼ cup plus 2 tablespoons all-purpose flour

¼ teaspoon freshly grated nutmeg

Coarse salt

1 Bring milk to a gentle simmer in a small saucepan over low heat. Melt butter in a medium saucepan over medium. Whisk in flour. Reduce heat to low, and cook, whisking often, 3 minutes (do not let flour brown).

2 Gradually add hot milk into the butter mixture, whisking constantly to prevent lumps from forming. Add nutmeg and season with salt.

3 Bring to a boil, whisking constantly. Cook, whisking, until thickened, about 10 minutes. Reduce heat to low, and cook until the raw flour taste is gone, 5 to 10 minutes more. Let cool slightly before using. Sauce can be refrigerated, covered, up to 5 days; let cool completely before storing.

MAKES 6 CUPS

Per serving (½ cup): 125 calories, 8.12 g fat (5.14 g saturated fat), 24.81 mg cholesterol, 8.69 g carbohydrates, 4.49 g protein, 0.11 g fiber

TOMATO SAUCE

2 cans (28 ounces each) whole peeled plum tomatoes with juice

3 garlic cloves, coarsely chopped

¼ cup extra-virgin olive oil

Coarse salt and freshly ground pepper

1 Pulse tomatoes and their juices in a food processor until coarsely chopped.

2 Heat garlic and olive oil in a 5-quart pot over medium until garlic begins to sizzle, about 2 minutes. Add tomato puree, season with salt and pepper, and bring to a boil. Reduce heat, and simmer, partially covered and stirring occasionally, 30 minutes. Season with salt and pepper. Sauce can be refrigerated up to 1 week or frozen up to 1 month in an airtight container.

MAKES 6 CUPS

V G S Per serving (½ cup): 63 calories, 4.68 g fat (0.65 g saturated fat), 0 mg cholesterol, 5.54 g carbohydrates, 1.08 g protein, 1.34 g fiber

PIZZA SAUCE

¼ cup olive oil

2 cans (28 ounces each) whole peeled tomatoes

1½ teaspoons dried oregano

Coarse salt and freshly ground pepper

1 Heat olive oil in a large skillet over medium. Using your hands, crush tomatoes into a bowl, then add to skillet along with oregano. Season with salt and pepper. Cook over medium-low heat, breaking up tomatoes with a spoon, until sauce has thickened, 40 to 50 minutes.

2 For a smooth sauce, pass it through a food mill, or press through a fine sieve into a large bowl; discard solids. Let cool slightly before using. Sauce can be refrigerated up to 1 week or frozen up to 1 month in an airtight container.

MAKES ABOUT 4 CUPS

V G S Per serving (¼ cup): 53 calories, 3.5 g fat (0.47 g saturated fat), 0 mg cholesterol, 3.87 g carbohydrates, 0.77 g protein, 0.85 g fiber

TOMATO-JALAPEÑO ENCHILADA SAUCE

1   can (28 ounces) whole peeled
     tomatoes, drained

½   white onion, diced (about 1 cup)

1   jalapeño chile, quartered (ribs and seeds
     removed for less heat if desired)

     Coarse salt and freshly ground pepper

1   tablespoon canola or safflower oil

¼   cup fresh thyme leaves

1   teaspoon white vinegar

     Pinch of sugar

1   Puree tomatoes, onion, and jalapeño
     in a blender until smooth. Season with
salt and pepper.

2   In a medium pot, heat oil over high until
     shimmering. Add tomato mixture and
simmer, stirring, until thickened, 5 to 10 minutes.
Remove from heat and stir in thyme, vinegar,
and sugar. Season with salt and pepper. Sauce
can be refrigerated in an airtight container
up to 4 days; let cool completely before storing.

MAKES 2½ CUPS

Ⓥ Ⓖ Ⓢ Per serving (¼ cup): 42 calories, 2 g fat (0 g saturated
fat), 0 mg cholesterol, 6 g carbohydrates, 1 g protein, 2 g fiber

ROASTED TOMATO SAUCE

1   pint cherry tomatoes (14 ounces)

1   tablespoon olive oil

     Coarse salt and freshly ground pepper

1   teaspoon balsamic vinegar

Preheat oven to 400°F. Arrange tomatoes in a
9-by-13-inch baking dish. Drizzle with the
olive oil and season with salt and pepper. Toss
to combine and roast in an even layer until
tomatoes start to burst, 20 to 25 minutes. Transfer
tomatoes and juices to a bowl and stir in balsamic
vinegar. Serve warm or at room temperature.

MAKES 1½ CUPS

Ⓥ Ⓖ Ⓢ Per serving (¼ cup): 24 calories, 0 g fat, 0 mg
cholesterol, 6 g carbohydrates, 2 g protein, 2 g fiber

PICO DE GALLO

3   tomatoes, cored and diced

½   cup finely chopped red onion

½   cup chopped fresh cilantro

1   jalapeño, ribs and seeds removed,
     finely chopped

     Juice of 1 lime

     Coarse salt

Combine ingredients in a bowl, seasoning with
salt to taste.

MAKES 3 CUPS

Ⓥ Ⓖ Ⓢ Per serving (½ cup): 19 calories, 0.16 g fat (0 g
saturated fat), 0 mg cholesterol, 4.2 g carbohydrates, 0.88 g
protein, 1.1 g fiber

TOMATILLO SALSA

2   tablespoons canola or safflower oil

1   small onion, finely chopped

3   garlic cloves, coarsely chopped

2¼   pounds tomatillos, husked and washed

1   fresh serrano chile (ribs and seeds removed
     for less heat if desired)

2   tablespoons coarsely chopped cilantro
     leaves

     Coarse salt

1   Heat oil in a saucepan over medium. Add
     onion and garlic; cook, stirring occasionally,
1 minute. Stir in tomatillos, 1 cup water, and
chile. Bring to a boil. Reduce to a simmer. Cover,
and cook, stirring occasionally, until tomatillos
have softened, about 15 minutes. Drain, reserving
¾ cup cooking liquid. Let cool slightly.

2   Working in batches (do not fill more than
     halfway), puree tomatillo mixture in a food
processor with reserved cooking liquid. Add
cilantro and season with salt; pulse to combine.
Salsa can be refrigerated in an airtight container
up to 3 days; let cool completely before storing.

MAKES ABOUT 5 CUPS

Ⓥ Ⓖ Ⓢ Per serving (½ cup): 62 calories, 3.86 g fat (0.34 g
saturated fat), 0 mg cholesterol, 6.96 g carbohydrates, 1.13 g
protein, 2.1 g fiber

YOGURT-GARLIC SAUCE

¾ cup plain Greek-style yogurt (2 percent)

2 tablespoons chopped fresh flat-leaf
   parsley leaves

1 tablespoon capers, preferably salt-packed,
   rinsed, and chopped

1 small garlic clove, minced

   Coarse salt and freshly ground pepper

Combine yogurt, parsley, capers, and garlic
in a medium bowl. Season with salt and pepper.
Cover, and refrigerate for up to 1 day.

MAKES 1 CUP

G Per serving (¼ cup): 29.5 calories, 0.85 g fat (0.56 g
saturated fat), 2.81 mg cholesterol, 2 g carbohydrates, 3.31 g
protein, 0 g fiber

TAHINI SAUCE

½ cup tahini (sesame seed paste)

   Grated zest and juice of 1 lemon

1 tablespoon olive oil

1 garlic clove, chopped

½ teaspoon ground cumin

½ teaspoon paprika

¾ cup water

   Coarse salt

Puree tahini, lemon zest and juice, olive oil, garlic,
cumin, paprika, and the water in a food processor
until smooth. Season with salt. Sauce can be
refrigerated in an airtight container up to 1 week.

MAKES 1¼ CUPS

V G S Per serving (¼ cup): 167 calories, 14 g fat
(2 g saturated fat), 0 mg cholesterol, 6.54 g carbohydrates,
4 g protein, 3 g fiber

CHILE MAYONNAISE

¾ cup mayonnaise

½ teaspoon Asian chile sauce (such as
   sambal oelek)

   Dash of toasted-sesame oil

Stir together mayonnaise, chile sauce, and
sesame oil in a bowl. Refrigerate, covered, up
to 1 week.

MAKES ¾ CUP

G Per serving (1 tablespoon): 57 calories, 4.91 g fat (0.72 g
saturated fat), 3.82 mg cholesterol, 3.51 g carbohydrates,
0.13 g protein, 0 g fiber

BASIL PESTO

1 garlic clove

½ cup pine nuts

4 cups fresh basil leaves

½ cup extra-virgin olive oil, plus more for
   pouring over top (optional)

1 cup grated Parmigiano-Reggiano (about
   4 ounces)

   Coarse salt and freshly ground pepper

In a food processor, pulse garlic and pine nuts
until coarsely chopped. Add basil and olive oil,
and process to combine. Add cheese and pulse to
combine. Season with salt and pepper. To store,
pour a thin layer of olive oil over the top, and
refrigerate in an airtight container up to 1 week.

MAKES 1 CUP

G Per serving (2 tablespoons): 229 calories, 22.72 g fat (4.11 g
saturated fat), 8.8 mg cholesterol, 1.95 g carbohydrates, 5.22 g
protein, 0.6 g fiber

HAZELNUT PIZZA DOUGH

Hazelnut meal can be purchased at gourmet markets or from online retailers; or make your own by pulsing toasted, skinned hazelnuts (see page 363) in a food processor until finely ground.

- 1 cup warm water (110°F)
- 1 envelope active dry yeast (1 scant tablespoon)
- 3 tablespoons extra-virgin olive oil, plus more for bowl
- 2½ cups all-purpose flour, plus more for surface and hands
- ½ cup hazelnut meal
- 1 tablespoon finely chopped fresh sage leaves

  Coarse salt

1. Stir together the water and yeast in a large bowl; let stand until foamy, about 5 minutes. Stir in oil. Add flour, hazelnut meal, sage, and 1½ teaspoons salt; stir until dough forms. Turn out onto a floured surface, and knead with floured hands until smooth.

2. Transfer to an oiled bowl, turning to coat. Cover bowl with plastic wrap, and let rise in a warm, draft-free place until dough has doubled in volume, about 1 hour. Divide dough into two balls. Dough can be wrapped in plastic and refrigerated overnight or frozen up to 3 months. Thaw frozen dough overnight in refrigerator before using.

MAKES ENOUGH FOR TWO 9½-INCH PIZZAS

HAZELNUT PASTRY DOUGH

You'll have one portion of dough left over after making the cauliflower tart (on page 252); it's great for apple or pumpkin pie (just shape it into a disk instead of a rectangle). To make regular pie dough, omit the hazelnuts and increase the amount of flour to 2¼ cups; or substitute an equal amount of ground, toasted almonds, walnuts, or pecans for the ground hazelnuts.

- 1¾ cups all-purpose flour
- ½ cup ground toasted, skinned hazelnuts (see page 363)

  Coarse salt

- 1 cup (2 sticks) unsalted butter, cut into small pieces
- ¼ to ½ cup ice water

1. Pulse flour, hazelnuts, and ¼ teaspoon salt in a food processor until combined. Add butter, and pulse until mixture resembles coarse meal, about 10 seconds. Drizzle ¼ cup ice water evenly over mixture, and pulse until it just begins to hold together (dough should not be wet or sticky). If dough is too dry, add more water, 1 tablespoon at a time, and pulse.

2. Divide dough in half, and shape each half into a rectangle. Wrap in plastic wrap. Refrigerate until firm, about 1 hour. Dough can be refrigerated up to 3 days or frozen up to 3 months. Let chilled dough stand at room temperature for 10 minutes before rolling; thaw frozen dough overnight in the refrigerator before using.

MAKES ENOUGH FOR TWO 4-BY-13-INCH TARTS

GRAIN COOKING CHART

GRAIN	LIQUID AMOUNT (for 1 cup grain)	METHOD AND COOKING TIME	YIELD
Barley (pearl)	2 cups	Rinse thoroughly. Bring water and ½ teaspoon coarse salt to a boil; add grains and return to a boil, then reduce heat, cover, and simmer 35 minutes. Let stand 10 minutes.	3 cups
Buckwheat groats (or kasha)	2 cups	Bring grains, water, and ¼ teaspoon coarse salt to a boil, then reduce heat, cover, and simmer 12 to 15 minutes.	3 cups
Cracked bulgur wheat	2 cups	Bring water and ¼ teaspoon coarse salt to a boil, then pour over grains (do not cook); let stand, covered, 30 to 45 minutes.	2½ cups
Farro	1½ cups	Bring water, grains, and ¼ teaspoon coarse salt to a boil, then reduce heat, cover, and simmer 20 minutes. Drain excess water; return to pot and let stand 10 minutes.	1¾ cups
Millet	1½ cups	Toast grains in dry pan over medium heat 3 to 4 minutes. Bring water and ¼ teaspoon coarse salt to a boil, then add grains and simmer, covered, 15 minutes. Let stand (covered) 10 minutes more, then fluff with a fork.	2½ cups
Quinoa	1½ cups	Toast grains in dry pan over medium heat 1 to 2 minutes. Add water and ¼ teaspoon coarse salt and bring to a boil, then reduce heat, cover, and simmer 15 minutes.	2½ cups
Wheat berries	5 cups	Bring water, grains, and ¼ teaspoon coarse salt to a boil, then reduce heat, cover, and simmer 30 to 40 minutes. Drain off excess liquid.	2¼ cups
Basmati rice (white or brown)	1½ cups for white; 1¾ cups for brown	Rinse until water runs clear. Bring rice, ¼ teaspoon coarse salt, and water to a boil; simmer, covered, 15 minutes for white or 30 minutes for brown. Let stand 10 minutes.	3 cups
Long-grain brown rice	1¾ cups	Do not rinse. Bring rice, ¼ teaspoon coarse salt, and water to a boil; simmer, covered, 35 to 40 minutes. Let stand 10 minutes.	2½ cups
Short-grain brown rice	2 cups	Do not rinse. Bring rice, ¼ teaspoon coarse salt, and water to a boil; simmer, covered, 40 to 50 minutes. Let stand 10 minutes.	2½ cups
Wild rice	2 cups	Rinse well. Bring water and ¼ teaspoon coarse salt to a boil first; add wild rice, return to a boil, then simmer, covered, 45 to 50 minutes. Let stand 10 minutes.	2½ cups

suggested menus

Mediterranean Mezze

Charred Eggplant Dip PAGE 20

Stuffed Marinated Hot Red
 Cherry Peppers PAGE 14

Roasted-Tomato Tabbouleh PAGE 200

Roasted Potatoes with
 Romesco Sauce PAGE 27

Assorted olives

Tapas-Style Dinner

Bruschetta with Lemon and
 Green-Olive Relish PAGE 63

Gigante Beans with Feta
 and Greens PAGE 52

Tortilla Española PAGE 16

Artichoke Hearts Roman Style PAGE 51

Verdant Spring Dinner

Fresh Pea Hummus PAGE 23

Spring Vegetable Ragout PAGE 70

Basic Polenta PAGE 366

Strawberries tossed with
 fresh mint leaves

Summer Farmer's Market Lunch

Smooth Tomato Gazpacho PAGE 110

Wilted Summer Greens with Goat
 Cheese Bruschetta PAGE 60

Zucchini "Pasta" with Tomatoes
 and Walnuts PAGE 32

Fall Harvest Feast

Mushroom, Spinach, and
 Scallion Tart PAGE 244

Stuffed Acorn Squash
 with Quinoa and Pistachios PAGE 56

Roasted Brussels Sprouts and Grapes
 with Walnuts PAGE 351

Cheese plate with figs, sliced apples,
 and pears

Warming Winter Dinner

Vegetable-Barley Potpies PAGE 163

Roasted Beet and Carrot Salad PAGE 212

Broccolini with Lemon PAGE 335

Sunday Brunch

Frittata with Asparagus, Goat Cheese, and Herbs PAGE 82

Orzo Salad with Roasted Carrots and Dill PAGE 282

Green salad with All-Purpose Vinaigrette PAGE 362

Mixed fresh fruit

Autumnal Vegan Dinner Party

Spiced Butternut Squash Soup PAGE 145

Pasta with Roasted Cauliflower and Lemon Zest PAGE 298

Sauté-Steamed Swiss Chard PAGE 347

Dried fruit, nuts, and dark chocolate

Portable Picnic

Crisp Tofu Sandwiches with Peanut-Ginger Sauce PAGE 251

Golden Beet Slaw PAGE 344

Quinoa and Green Bean Salad PAGE 348

Backyard Barbecue

Double-Portobello Burgers with Roasted Tomatoes PAGE 263

Grilled Potatoes with Garlic-Herb Oil PAGE 313

Grilled Corn, Avocado, and Cilantro Salad PAGE 324

Asian Dinner

Summer Rolls with Carrot-Ginger Dipping Sauce PAGE 28

Shiitake Fried Rice PAGE 86

Baby Bok Choy with Chile, Garlic, and Ginger PAGE 340

Sprouted Summer Salad PAGE 203

Taco Fiesta

Rajas Tacos PAGE 240

Portobello and Zucchini Tacos PAGE 240

Brown Rice with Black Beans and Avocado PAGE 81

Mexican Creamed Corn PAGE 320

Lime sorbet with toasted coconut

acknowledgments

This book represents the efforts of a hard-working, dedicated team of people. First and foremost, a big thank-you to *Whole Living* food editor Shira Bocar, editor-in-chief Alanna Stang, and design director Matthew Axe, as well as the editors (past and present) who contributed recipes and ideas to the book. The magazine has cultivated a loyal audience of readers who share in its mission to put life and body in balance, and who list eating a conscious diet among their goals and aspirations. We are delighted to deliver this book to them.

Thanks also to the Special Projects Group at MSLO, particularly executive editor Evelyn Battaglia and associate editor Stephanie Fletcher, who, under the guidance of editorial director Ellen Morrissey, curated the inspiring selection of recipes and organized them into one practical and beautiful volume; and to former managing editor Lisa Waddle for keeping everything on schedule. To art director Jessi Blackham and former design director Deb Wood, who created the book's modern and captivating design, and to John Myers, who compiled all of the photographs.

Thank you to photographer Andrew Purcell and stylist Lucy Attwater, for providing many of the beautiful images in this book, and to the other talented photographers whose work appears on these pages (see the complete list, opposite), as well as to photography and research editor Anna Ross.

As always, thank you to MSLO's chief integration and creative director Gael Towey, creative director Eric A. Pike, and executive editorial director of food Lucinda Scala Quinn. Others who contributed to the book include Monita Buchwald, Denise Clappi, Alison Vanek Devine, Tanya Graff, Davida Hogan, Erika Preuss, Miranda van Gelder, and Jocelyn C. Zuckerman.

Finally, we thank our longtime partners at Clarkson Potter/Publishers for yet another book we are so very proud to publish together, including Rica Allannic, Amy Boorstein, Angelin Borsics, Emma Brodie, Doris Cooper, Derek Gullino, Pam Krauss, Maya Mavjee, Mark McCauslin, Donna Passannante, Marysarah Quinn, Patty Shaw, Jane Treuhaft, and Kate Tyler.

photo credits

SANG AN
pages 67, 80, 120

QUENTIN BACON
page 246

JAMES BAIGRIE
page 87

CHRISTOPHER BAKER
pages 92, 295

HALLIE BURTON
page 210

LISA COHEN
pages 75, 346

JOSEPH DELEO
page 226

JOHN DOLAN
page 349

TARA DONNE
page 313

DANA GALLAGHER
pages 140, 157, 250, 300

BRYAN GARDNER
pages 30, 34, 37, 76, 143, 144, 193, 209, 217, 242, 303

HANS GISSINGER
pages 58, 99, 153, 181

JONATHAN GREGSON
pages 132, 275

RAYMOND HOM
pages 22 (right), 71, 115, 119, 135, 198, 206, 258, 272, 292, 333, 337, 345

LISA HUBBARD
pages 46, 317

JOHN KERNICK
pages 84, 95, 169, 205, 222

YUNHEE KIM
pages 18, 29, 108, 116, 127, 139, 190, 238, 334 (left)

FREDERIC LAGRANGE
pages 45, 83

RITA MAAS
page 338

KATE MATHIS
page 314

JOHNNY MILLER
pages 21, 22 (left), 38, 41, 42, 50, 53, 57, 60, 61, 64, 88, 104, 107, 112, 128, 165, 170, 189, 197, 214, 218, 221, 225, 234, 237, 291, 306, 310, 321, 322, 330, 342, 350

MARCUS NILSSON
pages 54, 136, 186, 194, 201, 253, 280, 334 (right)

VICTORIA PEARSON
page 249

CON POULOS
pages 123, 124, 161, 173, 284

ANDREW PURCELL
front and back cover, pages 2, 6, 8–9, 12, 17, 26, 49, 62, 79, 91, 100, 101, 103, 111, 131, 146, 147, 148, 150, 154, 158, 162, 166, 174, 178, 182, 183, 185, 230, 231, 233, 241, 245, 254, 257, 262, 264, 265, 266, 268, 279, 283, 287, 288, 296, 299, 304, 307, 308, 318, 325, 329, 341, 352, 353, 354, 356, 360

MARIA ROBLEDO
pages 96, 229, 271, 276

ELLEN SILVERMAN
page 177

JONNY VALIANT
page 72

NATO WELTON
pages 33, 202

ANNA WILLIAMS
pages 25, 68, 213, 261

ROMULO YANES
page 326

index

KEY

V vegan   **G** gluten-free   **S** special diet

Note: Page references in *italics* indicate photographs.